Map legend

🚰	Water fountain or tap (for drinking)	┈┈	Cycling track
🚻	Public toilet	┈┈	Footpath or multi-use track
⛱	Picnic facility	▦▦▦	Railway line
✳	Viewing point	▬▬	Tram line
🗿	Monument	▬▬	Freeway
🏛	Museum	▬▬	Highway
⛲	Fountain (decorative)	▬▬	Primary road
🚌	Bus stop	▬▬	Secondary road
◼	Train station or tram stop	──	Residential road
✕	Railroad crossing	➡	One-way road
🅿	Carpark	▬▬	River or canal
▨	Park	▬▬	Stream or drain

Published by Fi Hanafiah 2020
Melbourne, Australia

© Fi Hanafiah 2020
All rights reserved. This book or any portion thereof may not be reproduced or used in any manner whatsoever without the express written permission of the publisher except for the use of brief quotations in a book review or scholarly journal.

First printing: 2020
ISBN 978-0-9941957-1-5

Book's website: facebook.com/marathonwalking. To order copies of this book, please see the instructions on the website.

A catalogue record for this book is available from the National Library of Australia

Disclaimer: Please note that the author and the publisher of this book do not accept any responsibility whatsoever for any error or omission, nor any loss, injury, damage, adverse outcome or liability suffered as a result of the information contained in this book, or reliance upon it. Since the marathon and other running/walking events can be dangerous and could involve physical activities that are too strenuous for some individuals to engage in safely, it is essential that a doctor be consulted before undertaking training.

Base maps © OpenStreetMap contributors (openstreetmap.org/copyright)
All photos by the author, except where credited in the photo credits at the back of the book.

This book is dedicated to Sofie and Andria, and my parents, Zainab and Abdul Rashid.

I acknowledge the Traditional Owners of the lands mentioned in this book and pay my respects to their Elders past, present and emerging.

Preface

I've walked dozens of marathons and I've written a book called 'Marathon Training For Walkers and Beginners'. In 2014, I started a group called the *Marathon Walking Community* in Melbourne. We have thousands of members and walk at least once a week all-year round. To make our walks more varied, I needed to find new trails all the time. Despite going to libraries and scouring the Internet for more trails, more often than not, I had to piece together my own trails.

Hence, this book was born. This book contains many of the trails that my group has walked since 2014. They share some common characteristics:
- They start and end within metropolitan Melbourne (with a few exceptions)
- Most are at least 8 km long, which is equivalent to 10,000 steps.
- They are all accessible by public transport at both the start and finish.
- They are flat, safe and rely on pre-existing paths or cycling tracks.
- They involve as few road crossings as possible.
- They include at least one public toilet and one drinking fountain along the way.

Most books that I've read tend to focus on the bushwalks around Melbourne. I hope that this book will redirect your attention to Melbourne's urban trails, which in my opinion, are equally fascinating and surprising in their own way. I had a great time mapping these trails and then testing them on my own or with my group. In particular, I would like to thank my group members who helped with leading some of our walks: Andrew Harrington, Bev McAlindon, David Dolly, Joanna Austin, Moiz Ahmed, Suzanne Duce, Caroline Thomas, Sharon Gray, Richard Arnold, Meg Watts, Natasha Maxine O'Reilly, Nicole Scott and Jean Ng.

Like all maps, the maps in this book will gradually get outdated and may contain minor errors. If you have any feedback, let me know at facebook.com/marathonwalking and I will address them in future editions. I am also compiling a second volume of maps as I couldn't fit all the maps I wanted into one book. Watch out for Volume Two soon!

And if you happen to be in Melbourne, do check our website (facebook.com/marathonwalking) and join us for a walk. I hope to see you at one of these trails one day!

Fi Hanafiah

Trails sorted by region

Map	Start / End	Page	Distance (km)	Type	Elevation (m)	No. of Traffic Lights
	CENTRAL					
01	The Tan	12	3.8	Circuit	4 to 34	0
02	Princes Park	14	3.2	Circuit	40 to 49	0
03	Albert Park Lake	16	4.7	Circuit	3 to 5	0
04	Yarra River Loop	18	12.0	Circuit	1 to 11	0
05	City to Docklands	20	10.1	Return	1 to 10	4
06	City to Como House	22	9.8	Return	1 to 27	3
07	Ten Gardens Walk	24	6.7	Circuit	1 to 35	3
08	City to Collingwood Farm	26	12.5	One-way	1 to 34	0
09	Kooyong to Collingwod Farm	28	7.7	One-way	1 to 34	0
10	Melbourne City Marathon	30	42.3	Circuit	1 to 83	16
	EAST					
11	Glen Iris Loop	32	8.1	Circuit	14 to 56	3
12	Fairfield to East Camberwell	34	8.6	One-way	6 to 83	3
13	East Camberwell to East Malvern	36	7.5	One-way	25 to 68	3
14	Blackburn to East Malvern	38	12.5	One-way	25 to 101	5
15	East Malvern to City	40	`14.0	One-way	1 to 32	2
16	Blackburn to City	42	25.7	One-way	1 to 101	7
17	City to Fairfield Boathouse	44	15.4	One-way	1 to 35	0
18	Fairfield to Ringwood	46	24.2	One-way	6 to 128	4
19	City to Ringwood	48	39.2	One-way	1 to 128	4
20	The Thousand Steps	50	7.0	Circuit	123 to 513	0
	SOUTH					
21	City to Station Pier	52	9.8	Return	1 to 11	5
22	City to St Kilda	54	8.6	One-way	1 to 31	9
23	St Kilda to South Melbourne Market	56	8.7	One-way	1 to 11	4
24	St Kilda to Webb Dock	58	16.0	Return	1 to 7	1
25	Fishermans Bend	60	13.5	One-way	1 to 10	5
26	St Kilda to Mordialloc	62	23.2	One-way	1 to 28	1
27	Mordialloc to Frankston	64	19.3	One-way	1 to 10	6
28	St Kilda Marathon	66	42.3	One-way	1 to 28	7
	WEST					
29	City to Footscray	68	8.3	One-way	1 to 10	8
30	Footscray to Williamstown	70	8.2	One-way	1 to 14	2
31	Maribyrnong River (one-way)	72	12.2	One-way	1 to 42	0
32	Maribyrnong River Marathon	74	44.0	Return	1 to 43	0
33	Williamstown to Altona	76	10.7	One-way	1 to 6	0
34	Altona to Seabrook	78	20.8	Return	1 to 7	0
35	Williamstown Marathon	80	43.4	Return	1 to 7	0
36	Werribee Mansion and Winery	82	14.5	Return	2 to 26	0
37	Woodend Winery	84	9.4	Return	567 to 630	0
	NORTH					
38	Boathouse to Boathouse	86	9.0	Circuit	5 to 49	0
39	Farm to two Boathouses	88	10.5	Circuit	2 to 49	0
40	Collingwood Farm to Dights Falls	90	7.8	Circuit	2 to 46	0
41	Collingwood Farm to CERES	92	13.6	Return	3 to 39	0
42	Triple Farm Walk	94	10.0	One-way	3 to 40	0
43	Fairfield to Heide Museum	96	19.8	Return	6 to 50	0
44	Zoo to Collingwood Farm	98	8.2	One-way	3 to 50	2
45	Zoo to CERES	100	11.8	Return	27 to 50	2
46	Zoo to Fairfield Boathouse	102	6.7	One-way	17 to 50	2
47	City to Zoo	104	9.0	One-way	1 to 37	6
48	Rushall Station to City	106	16.6	One-way	1 to 34	0
49	Rushall Station to Coburg Lake	108	8.5	One-way	27 to 58	0
50	Epping to Alphington	110	22.4	One-way	34 to 127	0
51	Alphington to City	112	21.4	One-way	1 to 48	0
52	Epping Marathon	114	42.6	One-way	1 to 127	0

Maps		page
01	The Tan	12
02	Princes Park	14
03	Albert Park Lake	16
04	Yarra River Loop	18
05	City to Docklands	20
06	City to Como House	22
07	Ten Gardens Walk	24
08	City to Farm	26
09	Kooyong to Farm	28
10	Melbourne City Marathon	30
	EAST	
11	Glen Iris Loop	32
12	Fairfield to East Camberwell	34
13	East Camberwell to East	36
14	Blackburn to East Malvern	38
15	East Malvern to City	40
16	Blackburn to City	42
17	City to Fairfield Boathouse	44
18	Fairfield to Ringwood	46
19	City to Ringwood	48
20	The Thousand Steps	50
	SOUTH	
21	City to Station Pier	52
22	City to St Kilda	54
23	South Melbourne Market	56
24	St Kilda to Webb Dock	58
25	Fishermans Bend	60
26	St Kilda to Mordialloc	62
27	Mordialloc to Frankston	64
28	St Kilda Marathon	66
	WEST	
29	City to Footscray	68
30	Footscray to Williamstown	70
31	Maribyrnong River (one-way)	72
32	Maribyrnong River Marathon	74
33	Williamstown to Altona	76
34	Altona to Seabrook	78
35	Williamstown Marathon	80
36	Werribee Mansion and Winery	82
37	Woodend Winery	84
	NORTH	
38	Boathouse to Boathouse	86
39	Farm to two Boathouses	88
40	Collingwood Farm to Dights	90
41	Collingwood Farm to CERES	92
42	Triple Farm Walk	94
43	Fairfield to Heide Museum	96
44	Zoo to Collingwood Farm	98
45	Zoo to CERES	100
46	Zoo to Fairfield Boathouse	102
47	City to Zoo	104
48	Rushall Station to City	106
49	Rushall Station to Coburg Lake	108
50	Epping to Alphington	110
51	Alphington to City	112
52	Epping Marathon	114

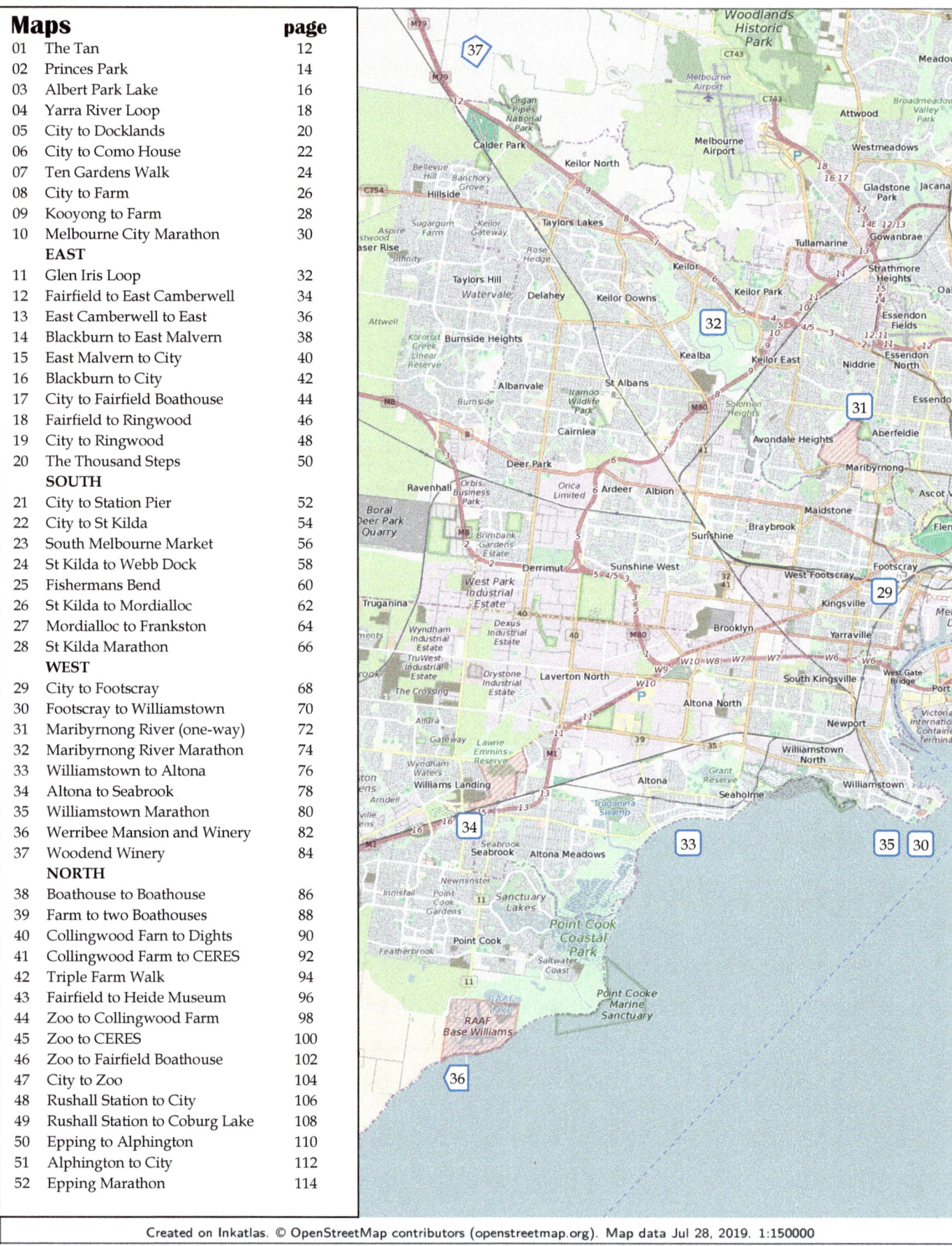

Created on Inkatlas. © OpenStreetMap contributors (openstreetmap.org). Map data Jul 28, 2019. 1:150000

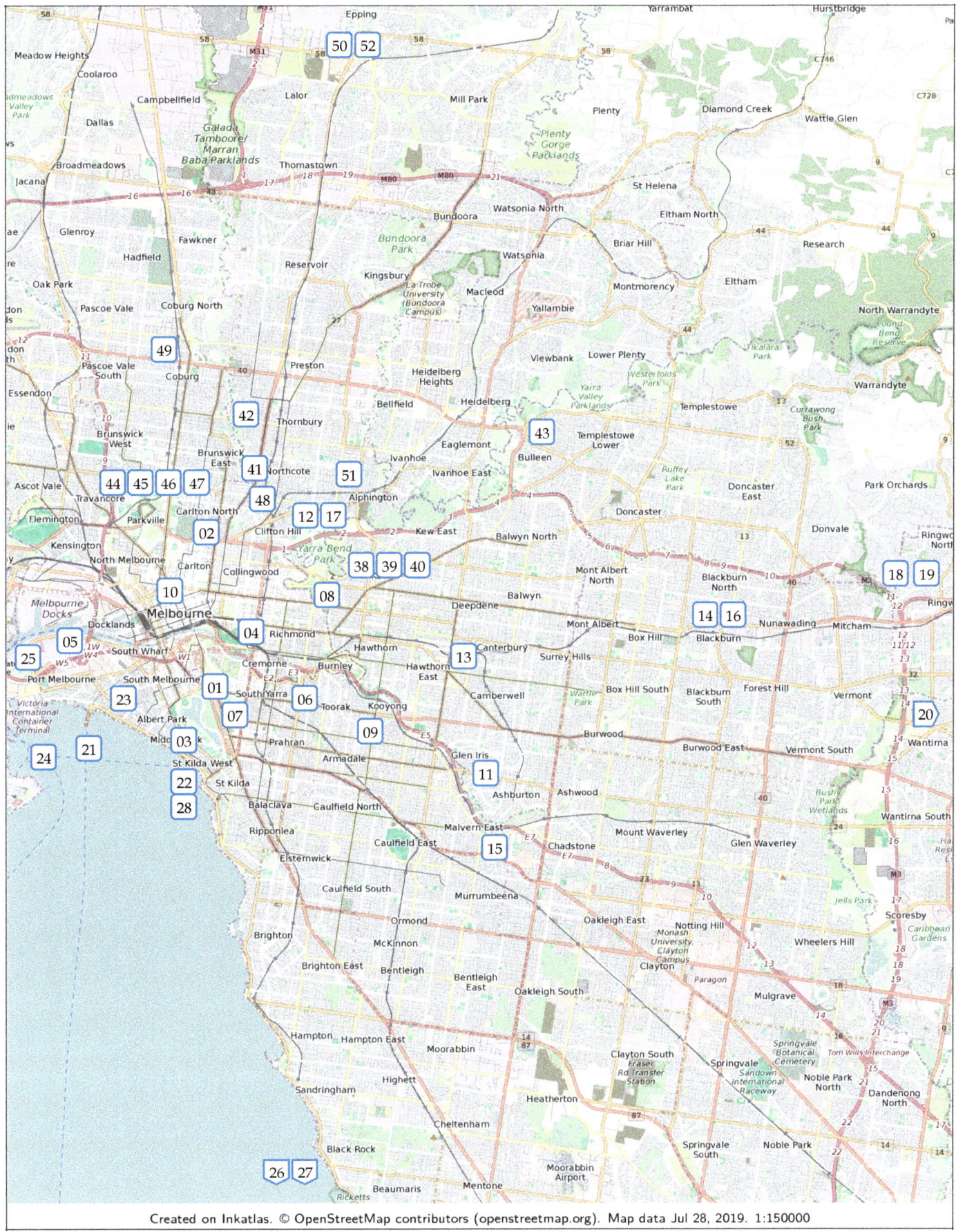

Trails sorted by distance

Map	Start / End	Page	Distance (km)	Type	Elevation (m)	No. of Traffic Lights
	SHORT DISTANCES					
02	Princes Park	14	3.2	Circuit	40 to 49	0
01	The Tan	12	3.8	Circuit	4 to 34	0
03	Albert Park Lake	16	4.7	Circuit	3 to 5	0
07	Ten Gardens Walk	24	6.7	Circuit	1 to 35	3
46	Zoo to Fairfield Boathouse	102	6.7	One-way	17 to 50	2
20	The Thousand Steps	50	7.0	Circuit	123 to 513	0
13	East Camberwell to East Malvern	36	7.5	One-way	25 to 68	3
09	Kooyong to Collingwod Farm	28	7.7	One-way	1 to 34	0
40	Collingwood Farm to Dights Falls	90	7.8	Circuit	2 to 46	0
11	Glen Iris Loop	32	8.1	Circuit	14 to 56	3
30	Footscray to Williamstown	70	8.2	One-way	1 to 14	2
44	Zoo to Collingwood Farm	98	8.2	One-way	3 to 50	2
29	City to Footscray	68	8.3	One-way	1 to 10	8
49	Rushall Station to Coburg Lake	108	8.5	One-way	27 to 58	0
12	Fairfield to East Camberwell	34	8.6	One-way	6 to 83	3
22	City to St Kilda	54	8.6	One-way	1 to 31	9
23	St Kilda to South Melbourne Market	56	8.7	One-way	1 to 11	4
	MEDIUM DISTANCES					
38	Boathouse to Boathouse	86	9.0	Circuit	5 to 49	0
47	City to Zoo	104	9.0	One-way	1 to 37	6
37	Woodend Winery	84	9.4	Return	567 to 630	0
06	City to Como House	22	9.8	Return	1 to 27	3
21	City to Station Pier	52	9.8	Return	1 to 11	5
42	Triple Farm Walk	94	10.0	One-way	3 to 40	0
05	City to Docklands	20	10.1	Return	1 to 10	4
39	Farm to two Boathouses	88	10.5	Circuit	2 to 49	0
33	Williamstown to Altona	76	10.7	One-way	1 to 6	0
45	Zoo to CERES	100	11.8	Return	27 to 50	2
04	Yarra River Loop	18	12.0	Circuit	1 to 11	0
31	Maribyrnong River (one-way)	72	12.2	One-way	1 to 42	0
08	City to Collingwood Farm	26	12.5	One-way	1 to 34	0
14	Blackburn to East Malvern	38	12.5	One-way	25 to 101	5
25	Fishermans Bend	60	13.5	One-way	1 to 10	5
41	Collingwood Farm to CERES	92	13.6	Return	3 to 39	0
15	East Malvern to City	40	14.0	One-way	1 to 32	2
36	Werribee Mansion and Winery	82	14.5	Return	2 to 26	0
	LONGER DISTANCES					
17	City to Fairfield Boathouse	44	15.4	One-way	1 to 35	0
24	St Kilda to Webb Dock	58	16.0	Return	1 to 7	1
48	Rushall Station to City	106	16.6	One-way	1 to 34	0
27	Mordialloc to Frankston	64	19.3	One-way	1 to 10	6
43	Fairfield to Heide Museum	96	19.8	Return	6 to 50	0
34	Altona to Seabrook	78	20.8	Return	1 to 7	0
51	Alphington to City	112	21.4	One-way	1 to 48	0
50	Epping to Alphington	110	22.4	One-way	34 to 127	0
26	St Kilda to Mordialloc	62	23.2	One-way	1 to 28	1
18	Fairfield to Ringwood	46	24.2	One-way	6 to 128	4
16	Blackburn to City	42	25.7	One-way	1 to 101	7
19	City to Ringwood	48	39.2	One-way	1 to 128	4
	MARATHONS					
10	Melbourne City Marathon	30	42.3	Circuit	1 to 83	16
28	St Kilda Marathon	66	42.3	One-way	1 to 28	7
52	Epping Marathon	114	42.6	One-way	1 to 127	0
35	Williamstown Marathon	80	43.4	Return	1 to 7	0
32	Maribyrnong River Marathon	74	44.0	Return	1 to 43	0

Before You Start

How do I find a suitable trail near me?

See pages 6 and 7 for an overview map of all the trails in this book. See page 5 to look up trails organised by regions (central, north, east, south and west). See page 8 to search for trails that are of a specific distance.

How do I interpret the maps?

All maps in this book are oriented with **north** pointing to the top of the page. The map legend is on the first and last pages of this book. The trail that you are doing is marked in red. The start of every trail is marked with a zero, signifying the zero kilometre mark. Each kilometre is marked on the trail in red.

Are the trails suitable for walking only or running as well?

All trails in the book are suitable for walking and running. Please note that most trails in this book include a few road crossings. If you are a fast runner who hates to stop at traffic lights, do choose trails with minimal road crossings or traffic lights.

What if I am training for a half-marathon (21 km) or 10 km distance instead of a full-marathon (42 km)?

All trails in this book can be easily shortened (or lengthened) to suit your 10K or half-marathon training. For example, a 15 km one-way trail can become a 10 km distance by going 5 km in one direction and then returning to the start. In addition, many of the longer trails have exit points such as train stations in the middle.

What if I am training for a full marathon or ultramarathon?

This is the main reason for this book's existence, as there are quite a few trails in this book which are over 42 km long. 42 km is the minimum distance you should be able to cover if you are preparing for a ultramarathon distance. All the one-way trails in this book can also be doubled in length by returning back to the start.

Do I need a car to get to some of these trails?

All trails in this book start and end near public transport (e.g. train, tram or bus). When I say 'near', I mean about 1 km or less, or about 10 minutes of walking. Many trails have access to public transport midway, so you can cut your walk short if you want to.

Are public toilets easily accessible on these trails?

Where available, I have indicated the locations of public toilets on the maps. All trails in this book have at least one public toilet along the way. However, some trails are so long that you may not be able to access a public toilet when you need to. Please be aware of this and plan accordingly. Tip: You can download free apps on your phone that can show you the locations of the nearest public toilets. Do a search for 'australia public toilets app' and there should be several options.

Must I bring water when doing these trails?

I have indicated the locations of drinking fountains or taps on the maps. Please note that drinking fountains become scarcer the further you are from the CBD. In addition, the drinking fountains that are marked on the maps might occasionally be under maintenance. Therefore, I recommend bringing a water bottle for any trail longer than 10 km. You should aim to drink water every 3 to 5 km, and more often on a hot day.

Do I have to cross roads?

Most trails in this book do have road crossings and I have listed the number of road crossings with traffic lights for every trail. Do note that some road crossings will not have traffic lights or pedestrian crossings, so take the usual precautions when crossing these.

What other safety precautions should I take?

If you're training alone, always let your family and/or friends know where you're going and how long you'll be away.

Second, bring a mobile phone, a public transport card and some cash at all walks. Get a running belt that can store all these things if you have no pockets.

Third, please check the weather and environmental conditions before going on a trail. The important websites to check in Melbourne are:
   (a) Weather forecast - Bureau of Meteorology website (www.bom.gov.au)
   (b) Bushfires and other emergencies - emergency.vic.gov.au
   (c) Floods - search for 'rainfall and river conditions' at www.bom.gov.au
   (d) Public transport disruptions - ptv.vic.gov.au
   (e) Road traffic disruptions – vicroads.vic.gov.au
   (f) Walking or cycling trail disruptions – parks.vic.gov.au. It is also advisable to check the local council websites in case of any construction works.

Please dress and equip yourself accordingly after checking these websites.

Night training

Generally, the trails listed in this book are NOT well-lit at night with the exception of the Tan (Map 1). If you have to train at night, do let friends/family know where you will be.

What to bring and wear

Longer trails (more than 10 km)

- Comfortable, worn-in shoes. Never wear brand-new shoes on a long walk!
- Sports socks
- Running belt – this is a good investment if you don't want to carry a backpack.
- Water bottle

- Mobile phone with Google Maps installed. Google Maps has a feature that broadcasts your location to a friend or family member.
- Cap/hat
- Snacks such as nuts, trail mix, or energy bars.
- Bandaids
- Bankcard or cash
- Public transport card
- Summer or hot conditions: Bring sunglasses and apply sunscreen generously.
- Winter or wet conditions: Light waterproof jacket
- Optional: GPS watch. Instead, you can use free smartphone apps to log your pace and location.

Shorter trails (10 km or less)

You might want to leave out the snacks. If there are sufficient drinking fountains on the route (check the maps in this book), you might want to leave out the water bottle as well.

That's it! Enjoy the trails!

Map 1 - The Tan

This is the venue of my walking group's inaugural walk so I'll put it as Map Number 1. I've even done an official marathon on the Tan (11 laps). I believe the Tan is the most popular track for walkers and runners in Melbourne. I once stood in one spot and counted 57 walkers/runners in one minute! The track is mostly gravel except along Anderson Street.

Distance: 3.8 km circuit. (If you want to be exact, there is a sign there that says it is 3.827 km)

Elevation: 4 to 34 metres above sea level. There is a 30-metre climb along Anderson Street that is good for hill training.

Start and end points: I have marked the starting point at the 'Pillars of Wisdom' near Swan Street Bridge because it is a common meeting point and there is a digital clock to help you time yourself. An alternative location for those coming from Flinders Street Station is to start near the Lady Janet Clarke Rotunda.

Getting there: Flinders Street Station (600 metres away). At least 7 tram services nearby.

Be alert: Road crossing at Government Drive. The Tan is lit from 5:30am to midnight, so it's the best and safest trail to do night training.

Try to spot: Lady Janet Clarke Rotunda, Queen Victoria Monument, Sydney Myer Music Bowl, Temple of The Winds, The Pillars of Wisdom, Guillfoyle's Volcano, Shrine of Remembrance, and the Observatory.

Lady Janet Clarke Rotunda (behind the trees)

Hill on Anderson St on the left

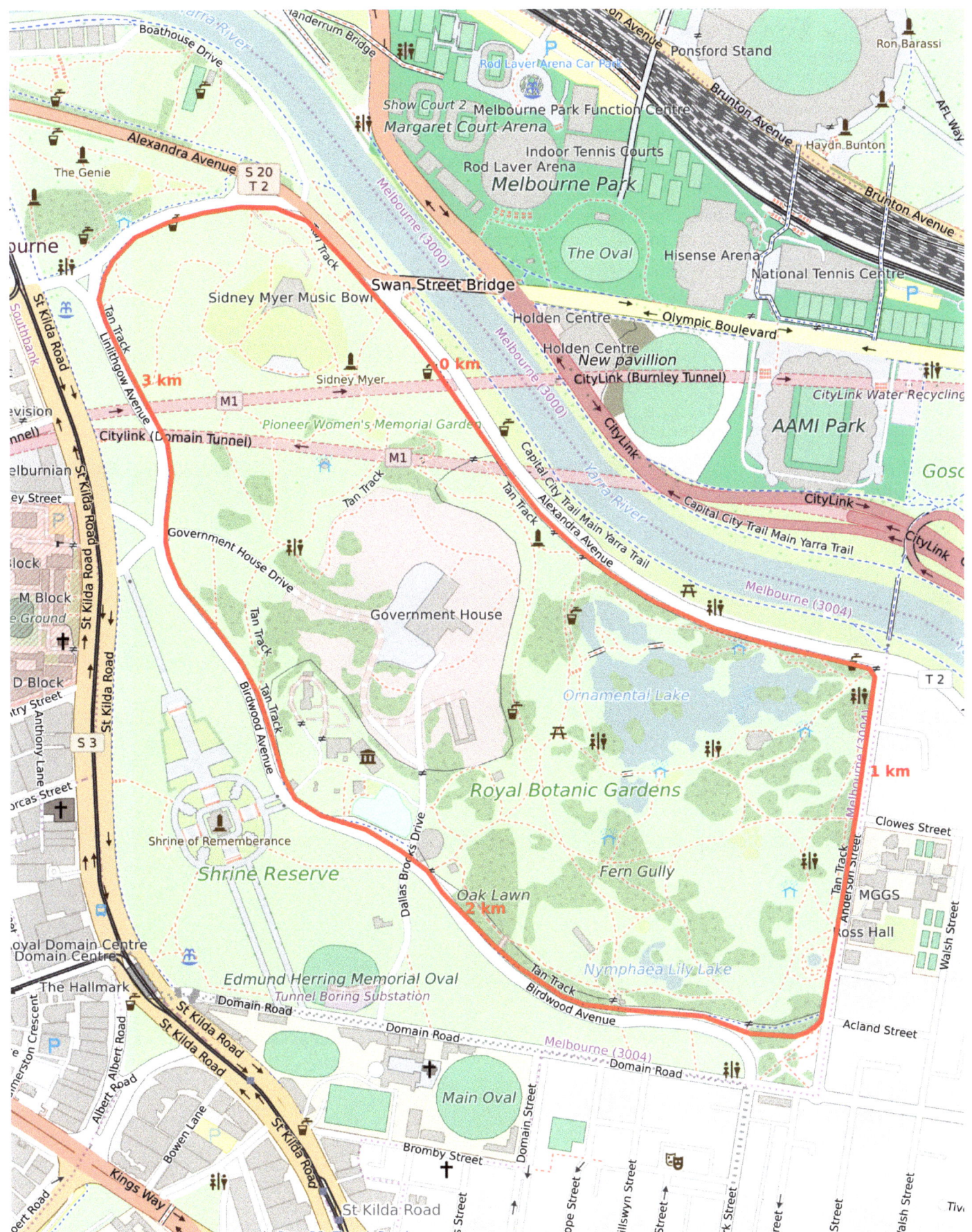

Map 2 - Princes Park

If you think the Tan is too crowded, you will love the relative serenity of Princes Park. The gravel track is easy on the legs and the paths are lined with mature river red gum trees. There are lots of drinking fountains and toilets. It also has a stadium, a few ovals, tennis courts and a bowling club. Melbourne University is to the south and the shops of Sydney Road are only 200 metres north of the start point. A marathon is held here every winter season so it's a good event to consider if you want to keep fit all year round. Fun fact: The inaugural match of the AFL Women's competition was held here in 2017.

Distance: 3.2 km circuit.   **Elevation:** 40 to 49 metres above sea level.
Start and end points: A convenient point near public transport, parking and a public toilet is at the northern end of the park, where the Capital City Trail cuts through the park.
Getting There: Jewell Station or Tram 19
Be alert: Car park entrances near the stadium and the bowling club.
Try to spot: Carlton FC stadium, Melbourne General Cemetery, Melbourne University and a sculpture called 'Within Three Worlds'.

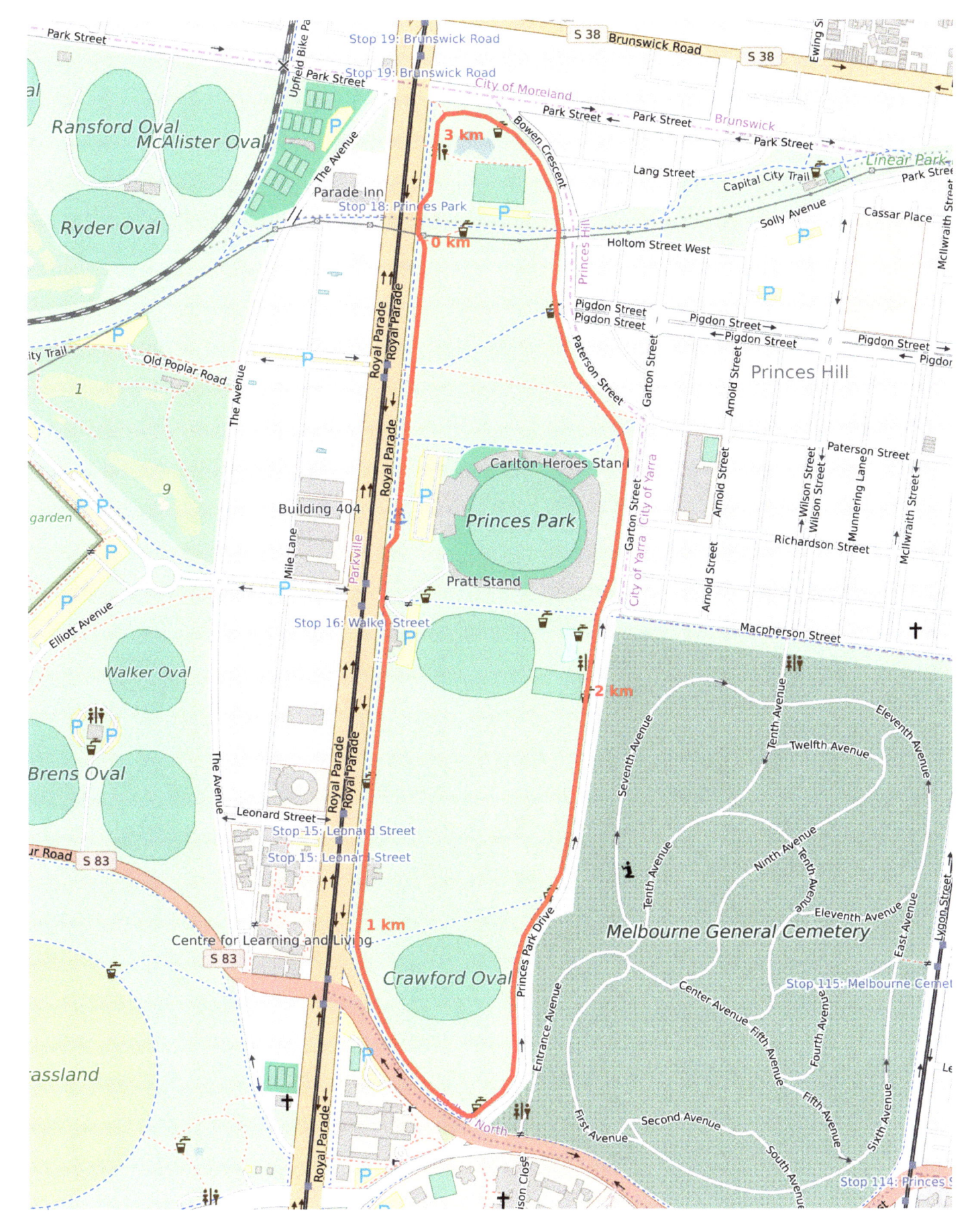

Map 3 - Albert Park Lake

This lake was originally a shallow lagoon in the delta of the Yarra River. Now it is a recreational park popular with cyclists, runners, walkers and rowers. The track is mostly gravel and there are great views of the city from the lake. Since 1996, Albert Park Lake has also been the site of the Australian F1 Grand Prix.

Distance: 4.7 km circuit.   **Elevation:** 3 to 5 metres above sea level.

Start and end points: If you're coming by tram 96, you can start near Carousel Cafe (see the zero kilometre mark on the map). If you're coming from the city, you can start near the Lakeside Stadium at the northern end of the park.

Be alert: Watch out for runners overtaking.

Try to spot: The Melbourne Sports and Aquatic Centre, the F1 Grand Prix grandstands and a beautiful view of the city's skyline. There are also lots of black swans and Pacific black ducks.

Map 4 - Yarra River Loop

The name of Melbourne's biggest river comes from an indigenous language term 'yarro-yarro', meaning 'ever-flowing'. This is a great walk if you like to be near water or to look at bridges. The trail has no road crossings so it's good for going fast.

Distance: 12.0 km circuit. **Elevation:** 1 to 11 metres above sea level.

Start and end points: Federation Square (near Flinders Street Station)

Be alert: Watch out for overtaking cyclists. Also keep in mind the turnaround points at MacRobertson Bridge in the east and Queens Bridge in the west.

Try to spot: Rod Laver Arena (home of the Australian Open), Herring Island, Royal Botanical Gardens, Government House and the 7 boathouses along Boathouse Drive.

Navigation tips: Start from Federation Square and walk eastwards on the north bank of the Yarra River. After 5 km you will pass under MacRobertson Bridge. Walk a further 100 metres, then turn left and follow Yarra Boulevard around and cross MacRobertson Bridge. When you reach the other bank, turn left and follow the cycling track again. Now walk westwards on the south bank until you reach Queensbridge St at 11.3 km. Cross the bridge and walk back to the start.

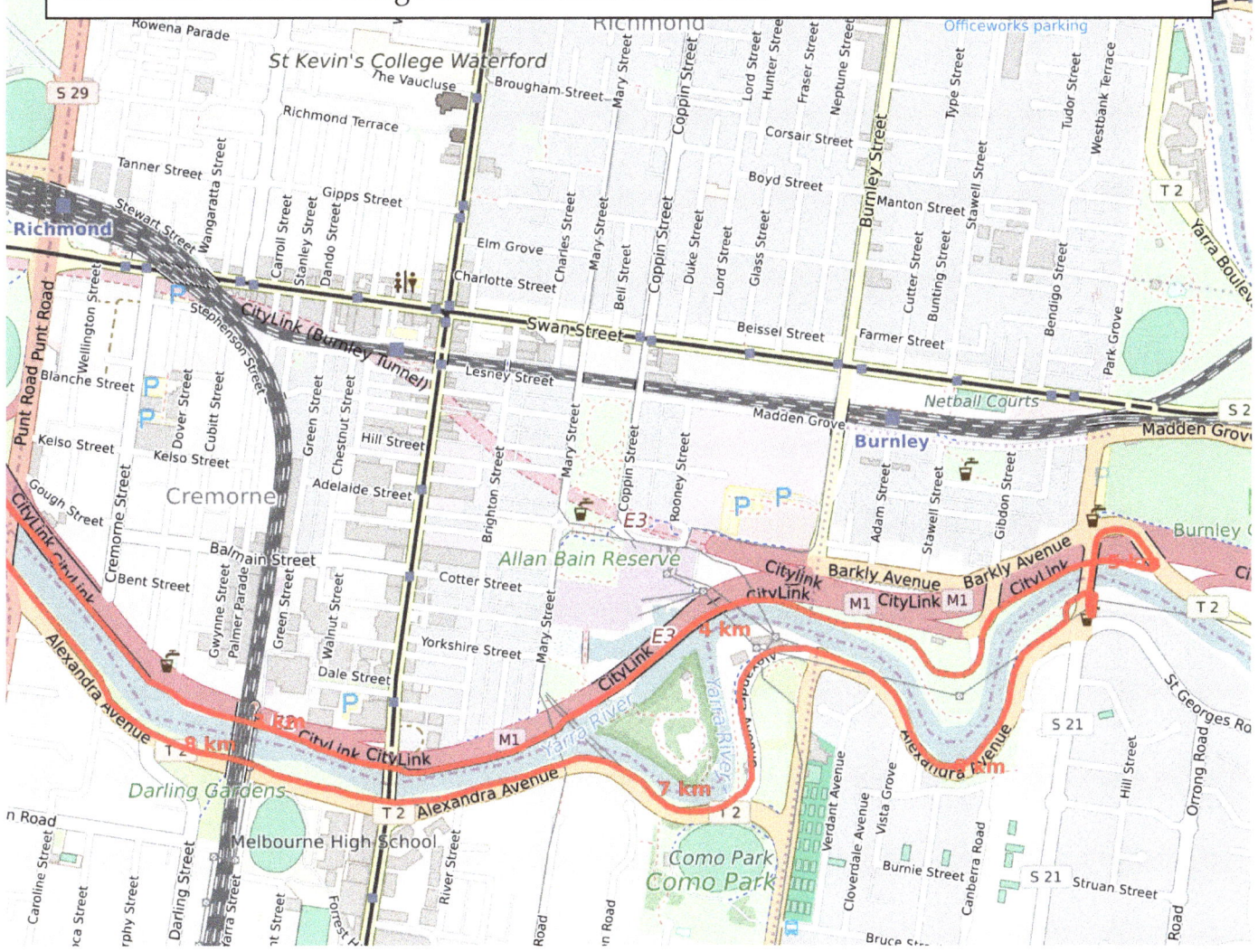

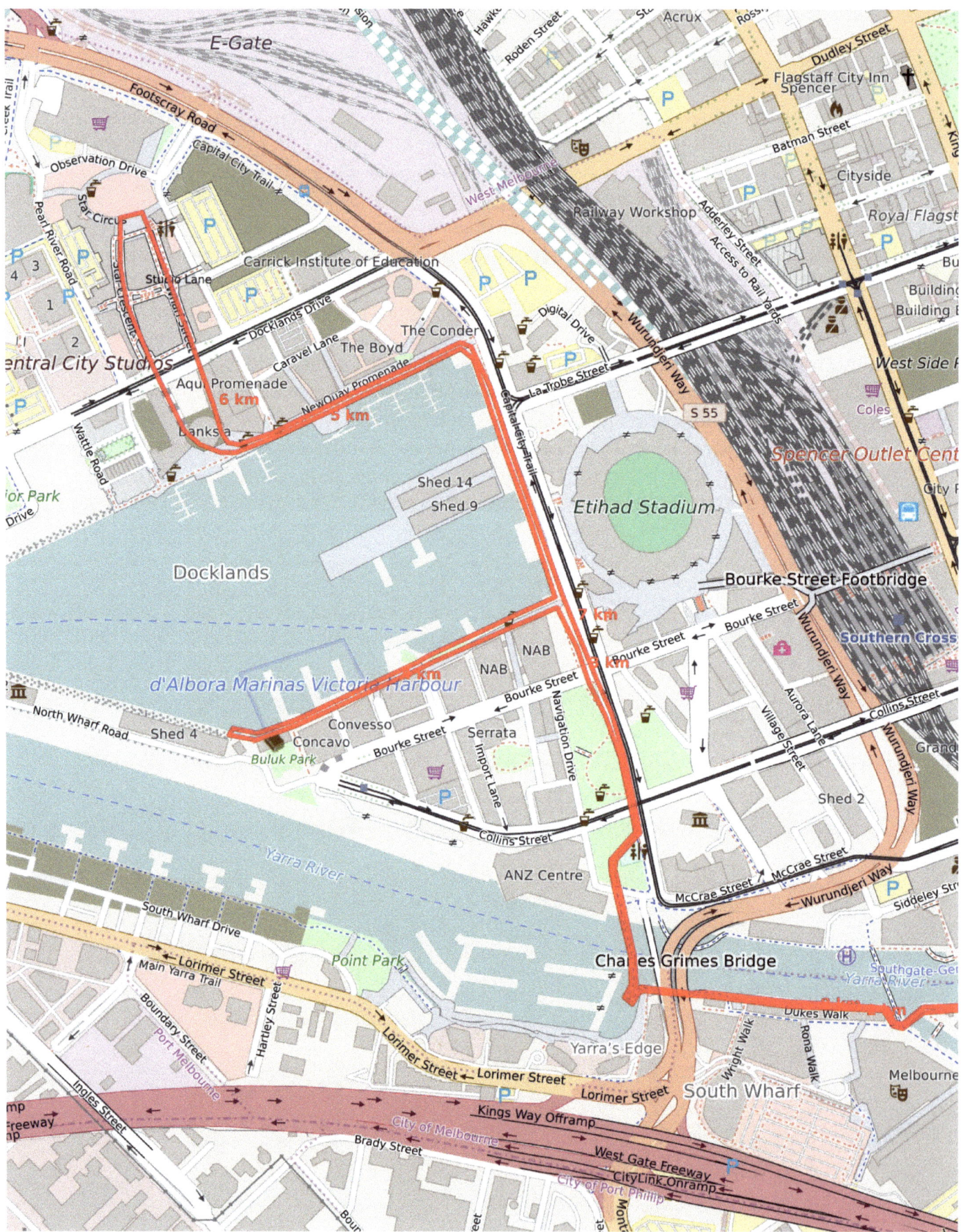

Map 5 – City to Docklands

The Docklands precinct has many things on offer for walkers – quirky public art, sea views, a ferris wheel and a stadium. I discover something new each time. One of my favourite landmarks is the Docklands Library, which is considered to be one of the most eco-friendly public buildings in Melbourne.

Distance: 10.1 km return. **Elevation:** 1 to 10 metres above sea level.
Start and end points: Federation Square (Flinders Street Station)
Be alert: Road crossings at Queensbridge St (traffic lights), Spencer St (traffic lights), Navigation Dr, Collins St (traffic lights), Bourke St (traffic lights)
Try to spot: The Melbourne Star ferris wheel, Marvel Stadium, The 'Cow In The Tree' artwork, Docklands Library
Navigation tips: Walk on the south bank of the Yarra River. At 2.4 km, cross the Webb Bridge to Docklands. At 3.1 km, turn left into Victoria Harbour Promenade. At 3.7 km, you will reach Docklands Library. Turn around and go back to Harbour Esplanade, and turn left. At 4.7 km, turn left into New Quay Promenade. At 6.0 km, turn right and walk towards the Melbourne Star ferris wheel (through Harbour Town Shopping Centre). Then return to the start without doing the Victoria Harbour Promenade section for a second time.

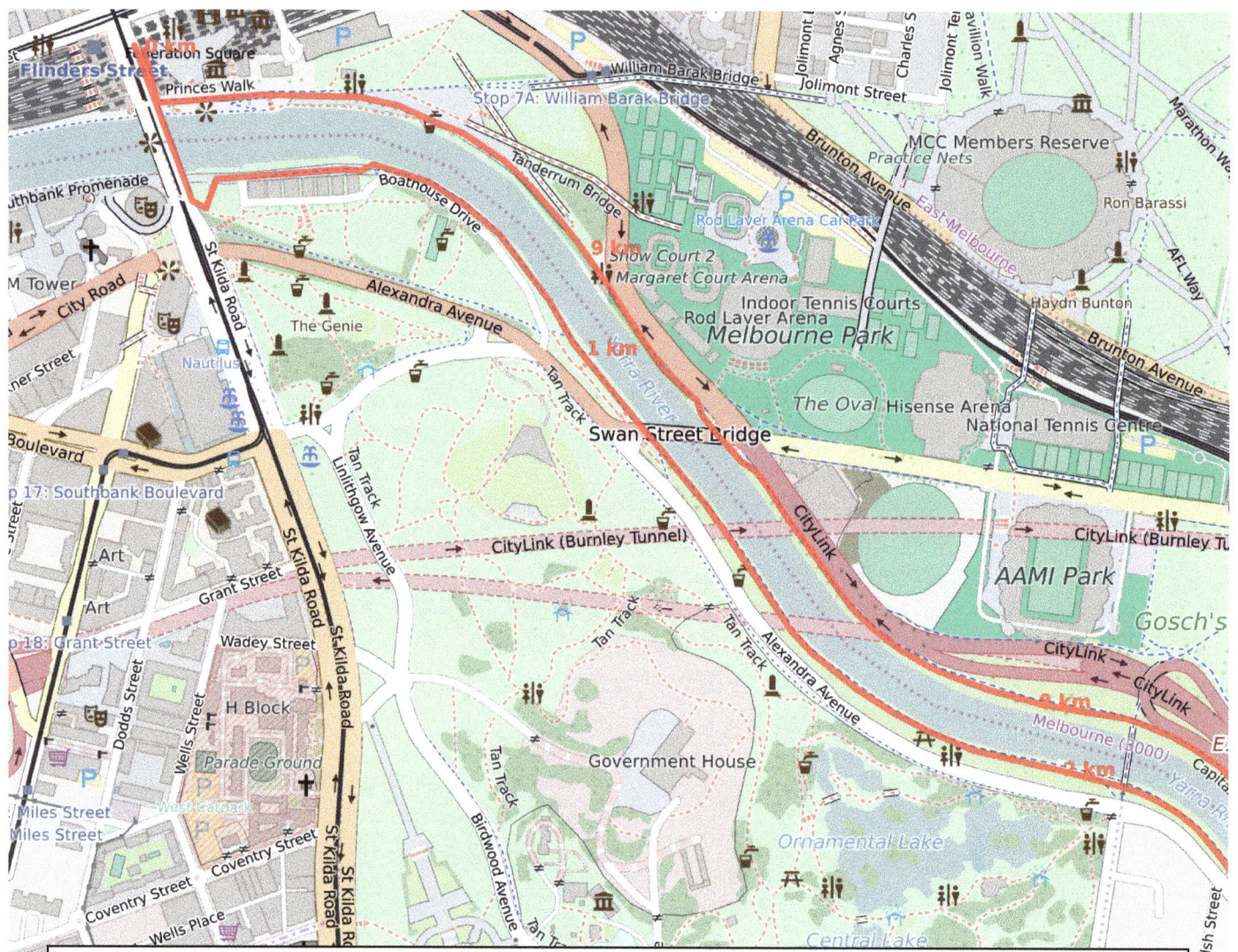

Map 6 - City to Como House

Como House is a heritage-listed building that was built in 1847 by Edward Eyre Williams. He named it 'Como' after Lake Como in Italy. The trail follows the Yarra River to Como Park, and Como House lies at the top of the hill there. Pack a picnic lunch to enjoy it in the grounds, if you have time.

Distance: 9.8 km return.

Elevation: 1 to 27 metres above sea level. Peak elevation is at Como House.

Start and end points: Federation Square (Flinders Street Station)

Be alert: Road crossings at Alexandra Ave (traffic lights), Williams Rd North (traffic lights), Williams Rd (traffic lights)

Navigation tips: From Federation Square, cross Princes Bridge and walk on the south bank of the Yarra River. At 4.2 km, cross 3 traffic lights in succession to get to Como Park. Como House is at the highest spot in the park. Go around Como Park and then return to Federation Square via the river again. On the way back, go by the north bank of the river for variety (cross the river at Chapel St).

Map 7 - Ten Gardens Walk

If you like gardens, you will love this walk! I like to do this walk in late spring to early summer, when the flowers are in full bloom. You will be taking lots of photos during this walk!

Distance: 6.7 km circuit.

Elevation: 1 to 35 metres above sea level. Peak elevation is at Guilfoyle's Volcano (at 3.6 km).

Start and end points: Federation Square (Flinders Street Station).

Be alert: Road crossings at Alexandra Ave (traffic lights), Southbank Blvd (traffic lights), Government House Dr, Anzac Ave, Birdwood Ave, Dallas Brooks Dr, Alexandra Ave again (traffic lights).

Navigation tips: First is Alexandra Gardens (at 0.5 km) with its boathouses. Second is the Queen Victoria Gardens (at 1.0 km) with its floral clock and many sculptures. Third is Kings Domain (at 1.5 km) which houses memorials to the police and 'Weary Dunlop'. Fourth is the Shrine of Remembrance Gardens (at 2.1 km). Next you head into the Royal Botanic Gardens and explore a few mini-gardens in there. The fifth garden is the Herb Garden (at 3.0 km), with a sundial in the centre. Sixth is Fern Gully (at 3.1 km) with its cool micro-climate. Seventh is Guilfoyle's Volcano (at 3.5 km). Eighth is the Arid Garden (at 3.6 km). Ninth is the Grey Garden (at 4.7 km), featuring grey-coloured plants from around the world. Tenth is the Pioneer Women's Memorial Garden (at 5.1 km), to honour the contribution of women settlers to Victoria. Cross to the north bank of the Yarra River and walk through Birrarung Marr to get back to the start.

Map 8 - City to Collingwood Farm

Established in 1979, Collingwood Children's Farm is considered the oldest children's farm in Australia. I just love the fact that there is a farm so close to the city centre. Try to time your visit to coincide with the monthly farmers' market.

Distance: 12.5 km one-way (25.0 km return)
Elevation: 1 to 34 metres above sea level. Peak is at 10.6 km.
Start point: Federation Square (Flinders Street Station)
End point: Collingwood Farm (900 metres from Victoria Park Station).
Be alert: This trail has no road crossings. Just watch out for cyclists.
Try to spot: Herring Island, a tiny vineyard near Young Street in Kew, and the Carlton & United Breweries buildings.
Navigation tips: Walk on the north bank of the Yarra River. Follow the main Yarra Trail eastwards. At 10.0 km, cross the footbridge. At 10.6 km, go left (west) when you reach Yarra Boulevard. At 11.3 km, leave Yarra Boulevard and take the left fork. At 11.4 km, cross the footbridge, go down the stairs and walk on the west bank of the Yarra. At 11.9 km, take the right fork. You will soon see the farm.

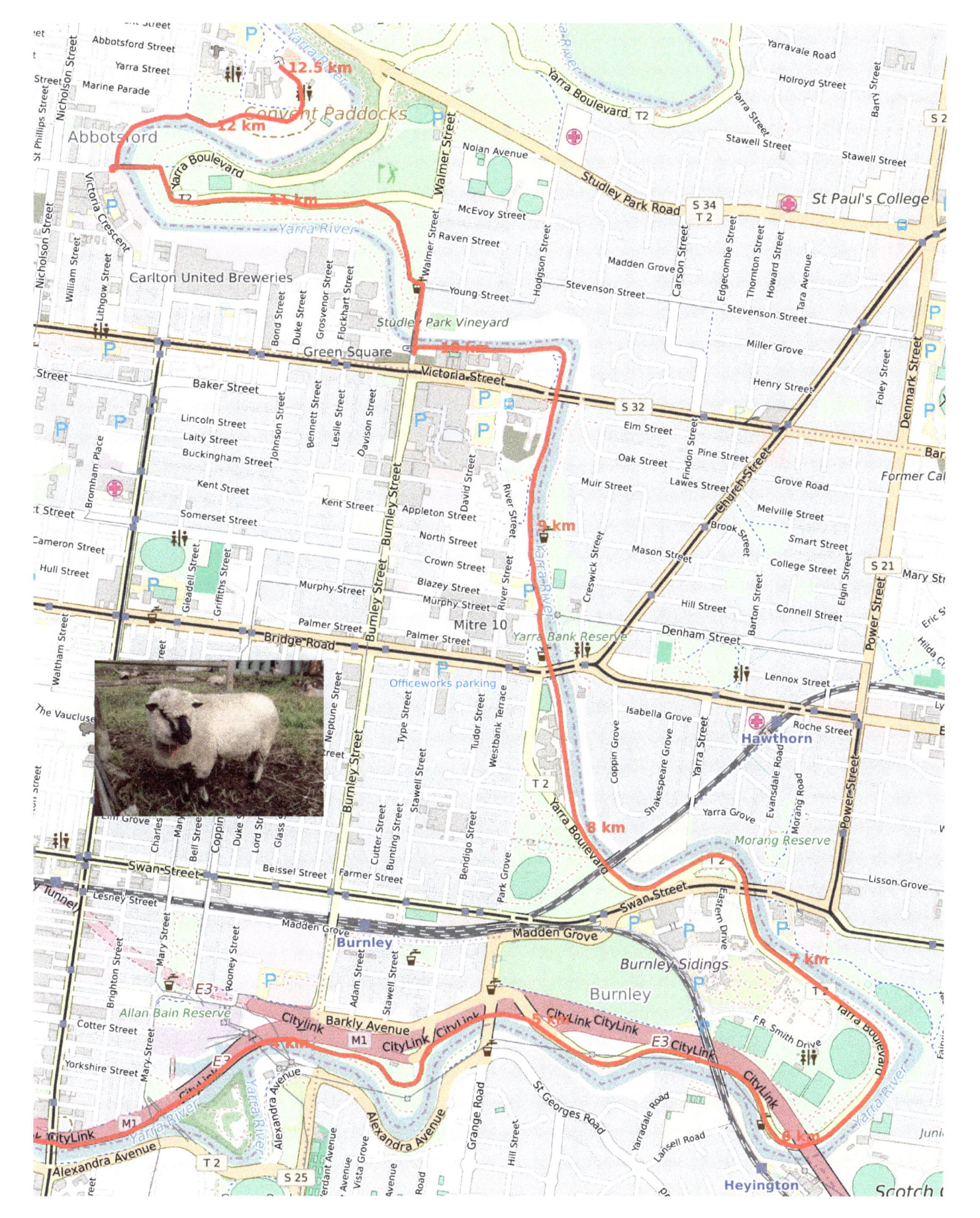

Map 9 - Kooyong to Collingwood Farm

This is a walk along a creek and a river. The trail approaches Collingwood Farm from the southerly direction instead of from Federation Square. At the start, you will walk past Kooyong Lawn Tennis Club, which is considered to be the spiritual home of Australian tennis. You will also find yourself on a cycling track that is suspended under the Monash Freeway for a kilometre.   **Distance:** 7.7 km one-way (15.4 km return).
Elevation: 1 to 34 metres above sea level. Peak elevation is at 5.8 km.
Start point: Kooyong Station.
End point: Collingwood Farm (900 metres from Victoria Park Station).
Be alert: This trail has no road crossings. Just watch out for cyclists.
Try to spot: Kooyong Lawn Tennis Club, a tiny vineyard near Young Street in Kew, and the Carlton & United Breweries buildings.
Navigation tips: From Kooyong Station, walk northwards along Glenferrie Rd and get onto the Gardiners Creek Trail under the Monash Freeway. At 1.3 km, you will cross the Yarra River, then go right. At 5.3 km, cross the footbridge. At 5.9 km, go left (westwards) when you reach Yarra Boulevard. At 6.4 km, leave Yarra Boulevard and take the left fork. At 6.6 km, cross the footbridge, go down the stairs and walk on the west bank of the Yarra. At 7.1 km, take the right fork. You will soon see the farm.

Approaching Collingwood Farm

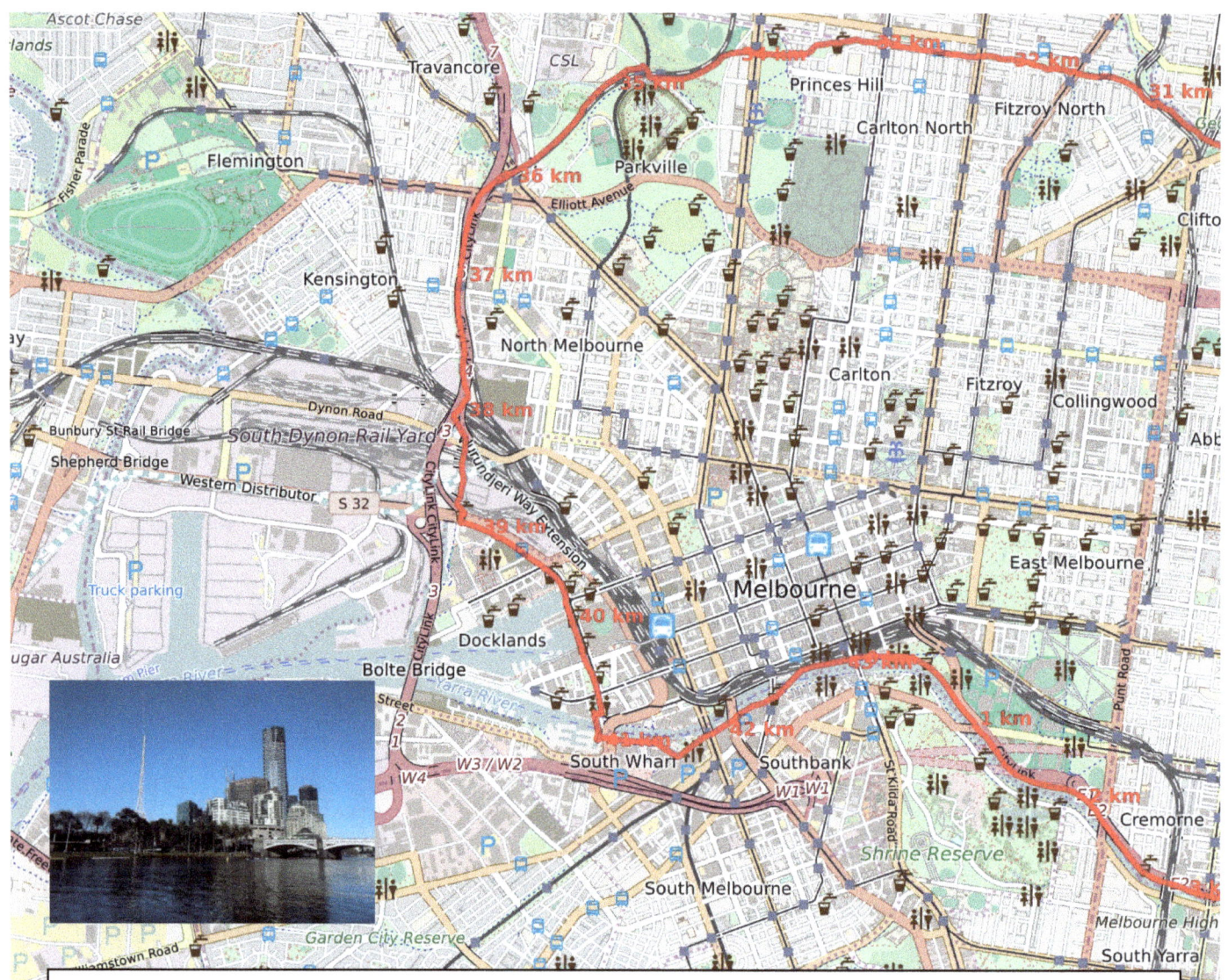

Map 10 - Melbourne City Marathon

I've been planning this trail for a long time. Melbourne already has the Capital City Trail but it is only 29 km long. Meanwhile, the annual Melbourne Marathon route uses busy main roads so it's not walker-friendly on a normal day. So I decided to put together a marathon-length circuit encircling the city. I call it the 'Melbourne City Marathon'. The western half uses the Capital City Trail, then it follows the Anniversary Trail to the east and returns to the city via Gardiners Creek Trail. To get detailed maps, study Maps 47, 46, 12, 13 and 15 in a clockwise sequence. Let me know when you complete this marathon!

Distance: 42.3 km circuit.
Elevation: 1 to 83 metres above sea level. Peak elevation is near Hawthorn East.
Start and end points: Federation Square (Flinders Street Station)
Be alert: See Maps 47, 46, 12, 13 and 15
Try to spot: See Maps 47, 46, 12, 13 and 15

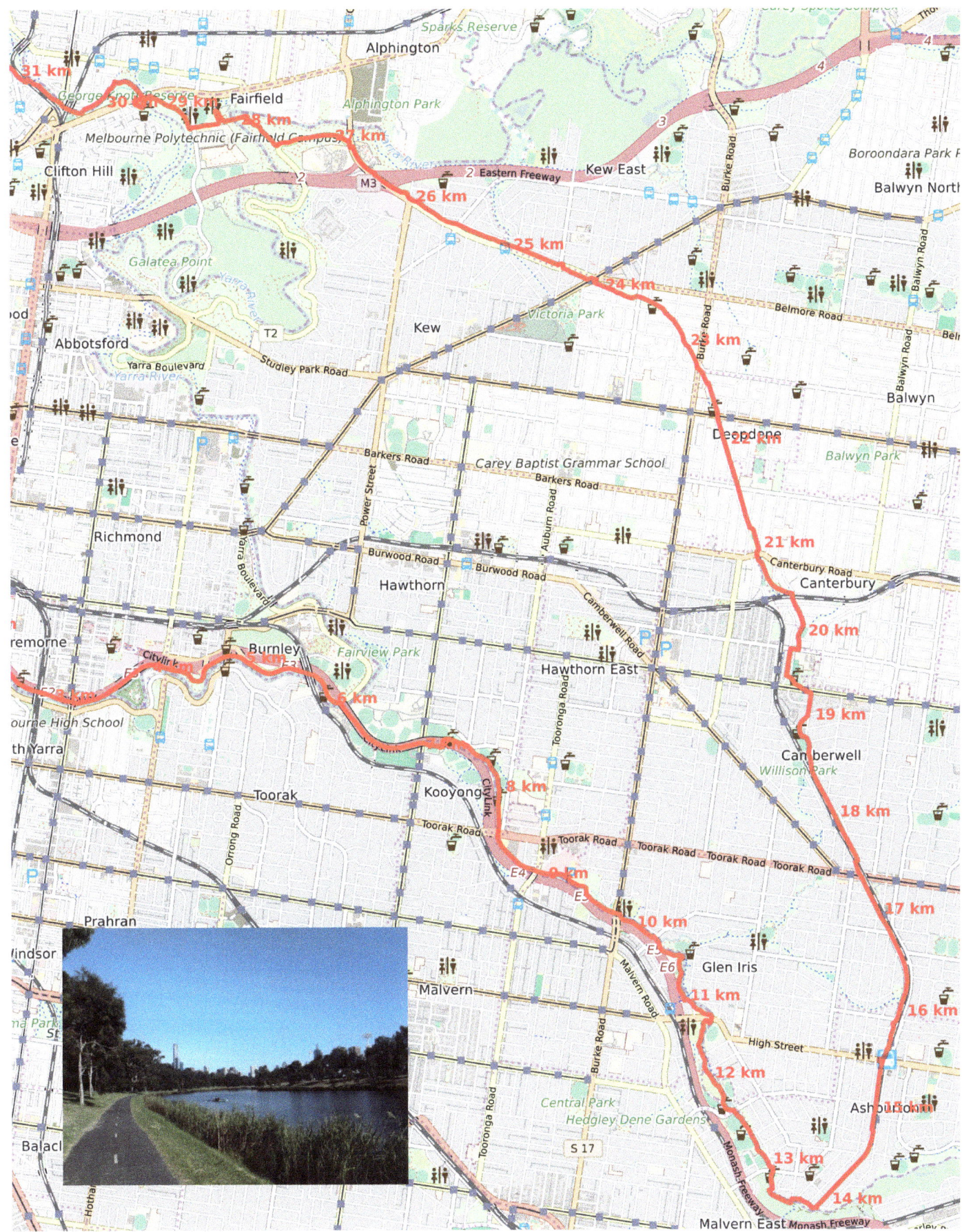

Map 11 - Glen Iris Loop

This trail goes through leafy suburbs and partly follows a disused train line. Called the Outer Circle Line, it stretched from Fairfield to the current Oakleigh Station. You will also use the Ferndale Park Trail which traces the path of the old Ashburton Creek.

Distance: 8.1 km circuit.

Elevation: 14 to 56 metres above sea level. Peak elevation is at 3.8 km

Start and end points: Glen Iris Station

Be alert: Crossings at Gardiner Parade, Glen Iris Rd, Wallis Ave, Ferndale Rd, Summerhill Rd, Florizel St, Prosper Parade, High St (traffic lights), Ryburne Ave, Winton Rd (traffic lights), Dunlop St (traffic lights)

Try to spot: the old rail infrastructure, and the current Ashburton and Alamein stations.

Navigation tips: From the eastern side of the Glen Iris Station, get on the overhead bridge and cross the Monash Freeway. Cross the footbridge over Gardiners Creek and go north. At 1.0 km, you will reach Ferndale Park Trail. At 3.0 km, you will reach the Anniversary Outer Circle Trail, so turn right (head south). When you reach High St, the traffic lights are about 10 metres to the side of the trail. At 4.4 km, the trail forks and becomes the Gardiners Creek Trail. Take the right fork (westwards). At 5.5 km, cross the footbridge over Gardiners Creek and take the right fork (westwards). You will criss-cross the creek a few more times before reaching the first bridge near Glen Iris Station.

Gardiners Creek

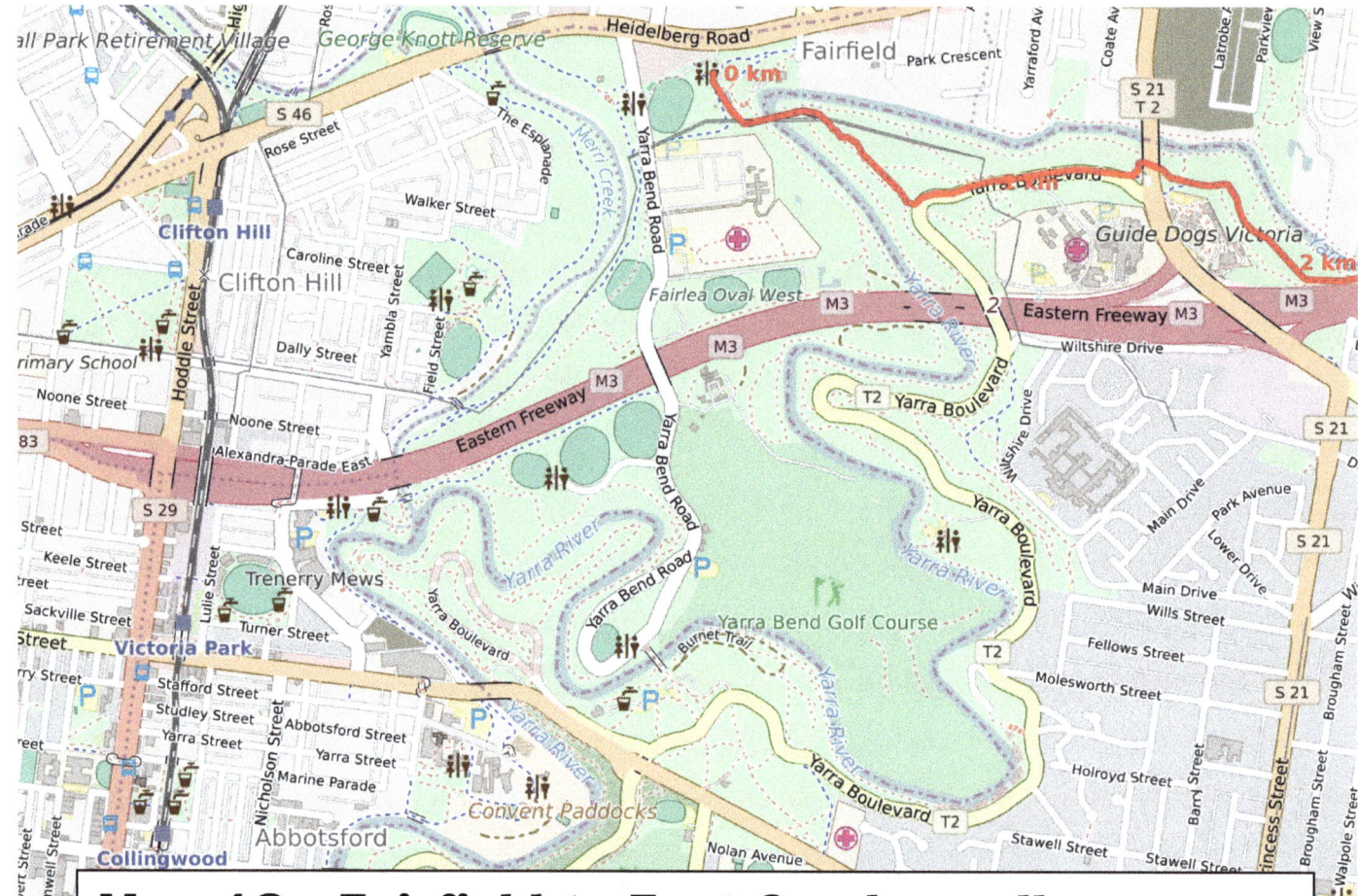

Map 12 - Fairfield to East Camberwell

This trail follows the disused Outer Circle train line. It starts from Fairfield Boathouse in its bush setting and meanders through the busy eastern suburbs.

Distance: 8.6 km one-way (17.2 km return)f

Elevation: 6 to 83 metres above sea level. Peak is at the 7.5 km mark.

Start point: Fairfield Boathouse (500 metres from Dennis Station)

End point: East Camberwell Station

Be alert: Road crossings at Kilby Rd, Connor St, Sutherland Ave, big roundabout at Belford Rd and Valerie St, High St (traffic lights), Normanby Rd, Argyle Rd, Burke Rd (traffic lights), Abercrombie St, Whitehorse Rd (traffic lights)

Try to spot: Fairfield Boathouse, Pipe Bridge, the old rail infrastructure

Navigation tips: Starting from the carpark near Fairfield Boathouse, cross the Pipe Bridge and climb up to Yarra Boulevard. Turn left (eastwards) and at 1.4 km go down the stairs to go under Chandler Highway. At 3.1 km, go through the tunnel under the Eastern Freeway. At 4.0 km, take the left turn at the crossroads (eastwards). You are now on the official Anniversary Outer Circle Trail. From now on, there will be lots of road crossings. There is a tricky crossing at the 6.4 km mark where the trail continues about 20 metres to the (east) side of the previous trail. When you see the train line above your head, East Camberwell Station is only 150 metres west of you.

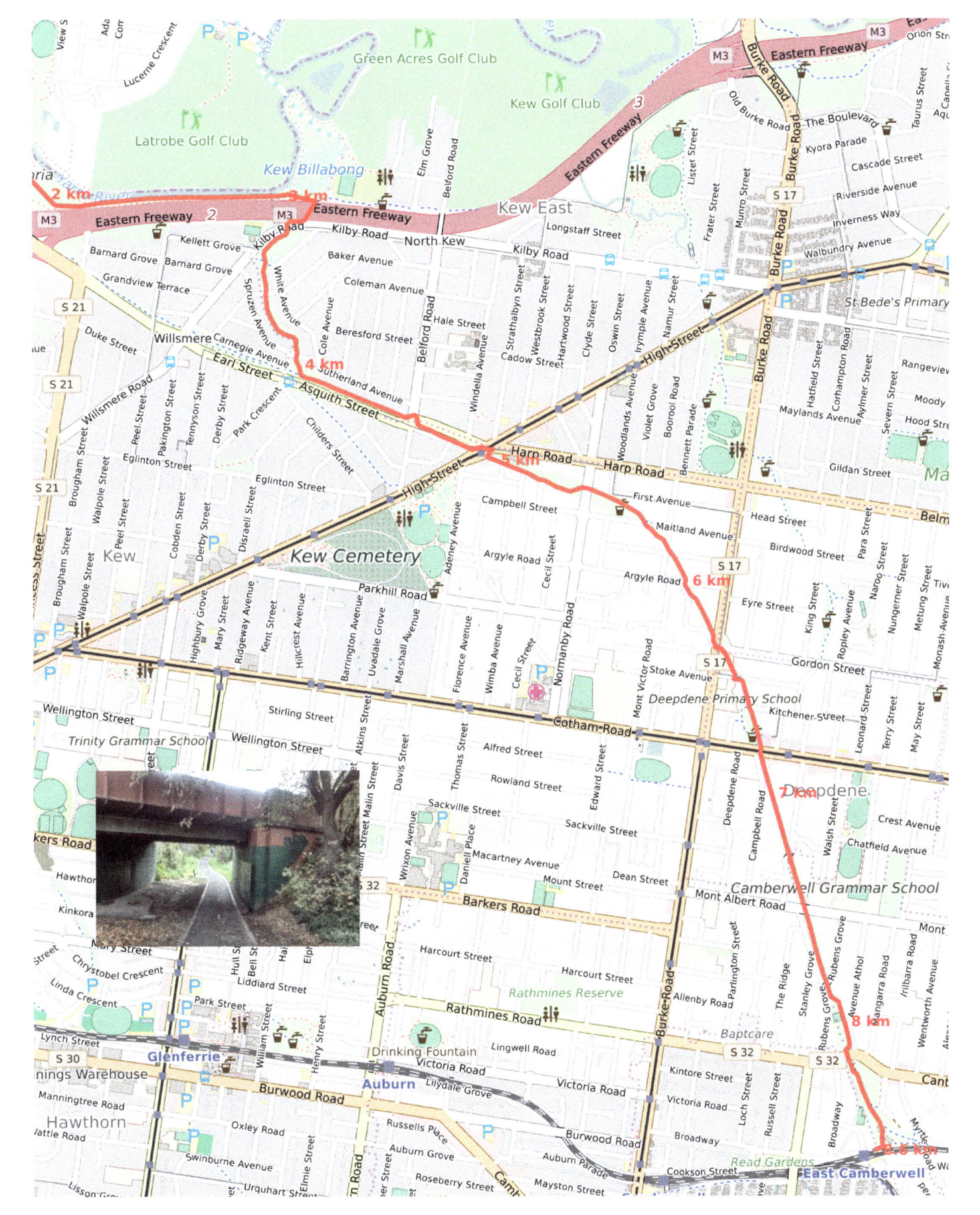

Map 13 - East Camberwell to East Malvern

Walk through a lush corridor that used to be part of the Outer Circle train line. This rail trail has several signboards describing the history of the train line. The Alamein train line runs beside most of the trail and you can enter or exit the walk at multiple points. This trail crosses a few busy roads but there are also many opportunities for café stops.

Distance: 7.5 km one-way, 15.0 km return

Elevation: 25 to 68 metres above sea level. Peak elevation is at the start.

Start point: East Camberwell Station.   **End point:** East Malvern Station

Be alert: Road crossings at Warburton Rd, Matlock St, Prospect Hill Rd, Riversdale Rd (traffic lights), Woodlands Ave, Shalless Dr, Culliton Rd, rail tracks at Bright St, Toorak Rd (traffic lights), Maverston St, Prosper Parade, High St (traffic lights), Ryburne Ave

Try to spot: Hartwell, Burwood, Ashburton and Alamein Stations.

Navigation tips: You will be following the Anniversary Outer Circle Trail for this walk. From the north side of Camberwell Station, go east 150 metres and turn right (southwards). The trail breaks at 0.75 km. So after crossing Prospect Hill Rd, go west 70 metres and then go south along Spencer Rd for 250 metres, then rejoin the trail. At 3.0 km, cross the railway track after Hartwell Station. At 3.2 km, cross Toorak Rd, where the traffic lights are about 30 metres west of the trail. At 5.1 km, cross High St, where the traffic lights are about 20 metres west of the trail. At 5.9 km, you will hit a fork. Take the right one (westwards). At 7.0 km, cross the footbridge over Gardiners Creek and take the left fork. Cross the Monash Freeway to East Malvern Station.

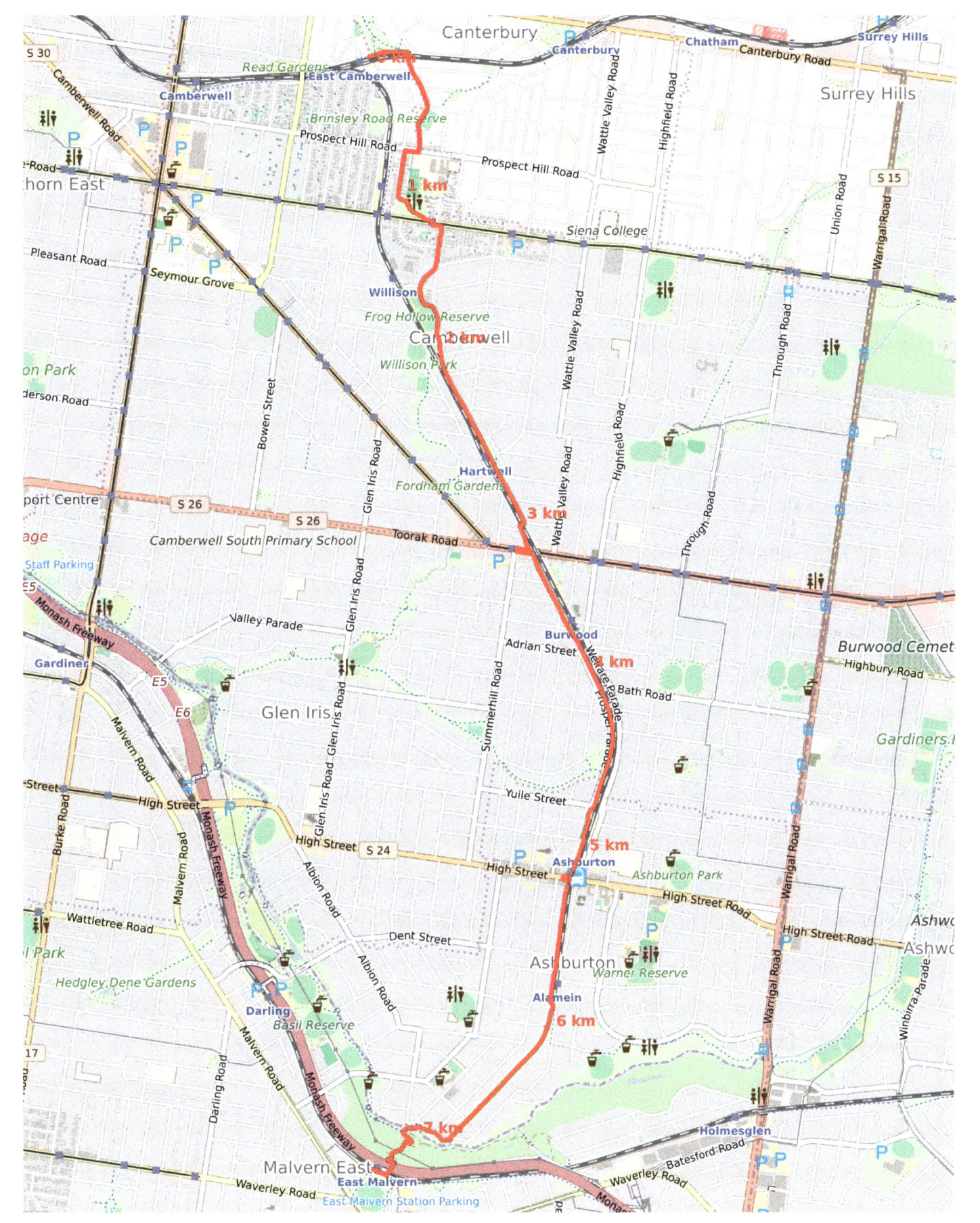

Map 14 - Blackburn to East Malvern

This trail follows the Gardiners Creek Trail most of the way. The creek is named after early settler John Gardiner who arrived in 1836. If you have time, do have a wander around Blackburn Lake before starting the walk.

Distance: 12.5 km one-way (25 km return)

Elevation: 25 to 101 metres above sea level. Peak elevation is at the start.

Start point: Blackburn Station.

End point: East Malvern Station

Be alert: Road crossings at South Parade, The Avenue, Main St, Pakenham St, Middleborough Rd (traffic lights), Albion Rd (traffic lights), Canterbury Rd (traffic lights), Riversdale Rd, Station St, Burwood Highway (traffic lights), Highbury Rd (traffic lights), High Street Rd, Ashburn Grove, Ryburne Ave.

Try to spot:. Deakin University Melbourne Campus and the site of the first drive-in theatre in Australia.

Navigation tips: From Blackburn Station, walk down Main St. At 0.7 km, cross Main St and head west along the Blackburn South Drain. At 1.8 km, cross Middleborough Rd and Albion Rd and head south. At 2.4 km, cross Canterbury Rd and continue with the path which is 100 metres to the west. At 4.0 km, turn right (westwards) and then go south to Station St. Cross Station St carefully (it's near a bend where cars can appear suddenly). At 6.0 km, you will reach Burwood Highway. Cross at the traffic lights which are 200 metres to the west. At 6.9 km, cross the creek and then cross Highbury Rd at the traffic lights. At 8.5 km, cross High Street Rd carefully (use the island in the middle) and rejoin the trail 50 metres to the west. At 9.7 km, the trail goes under Warrigal Rd. At 10.9 km, turn right (northwards) and walk along Ashburn Grove. After 150 metres make a hairpin left turn. At the 12.0 km mark, cross the creek and take the left fork towards East Malvern Station.

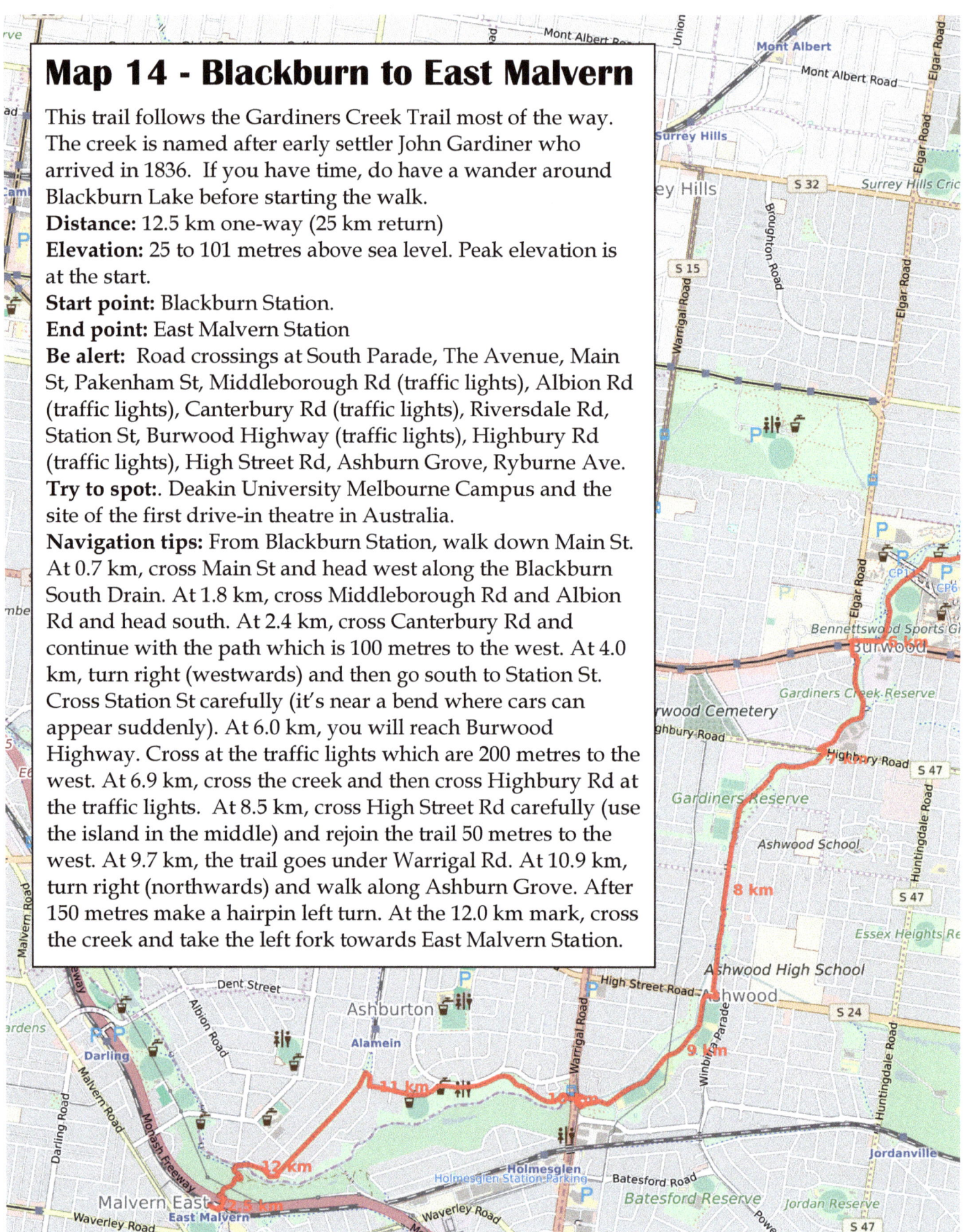

38

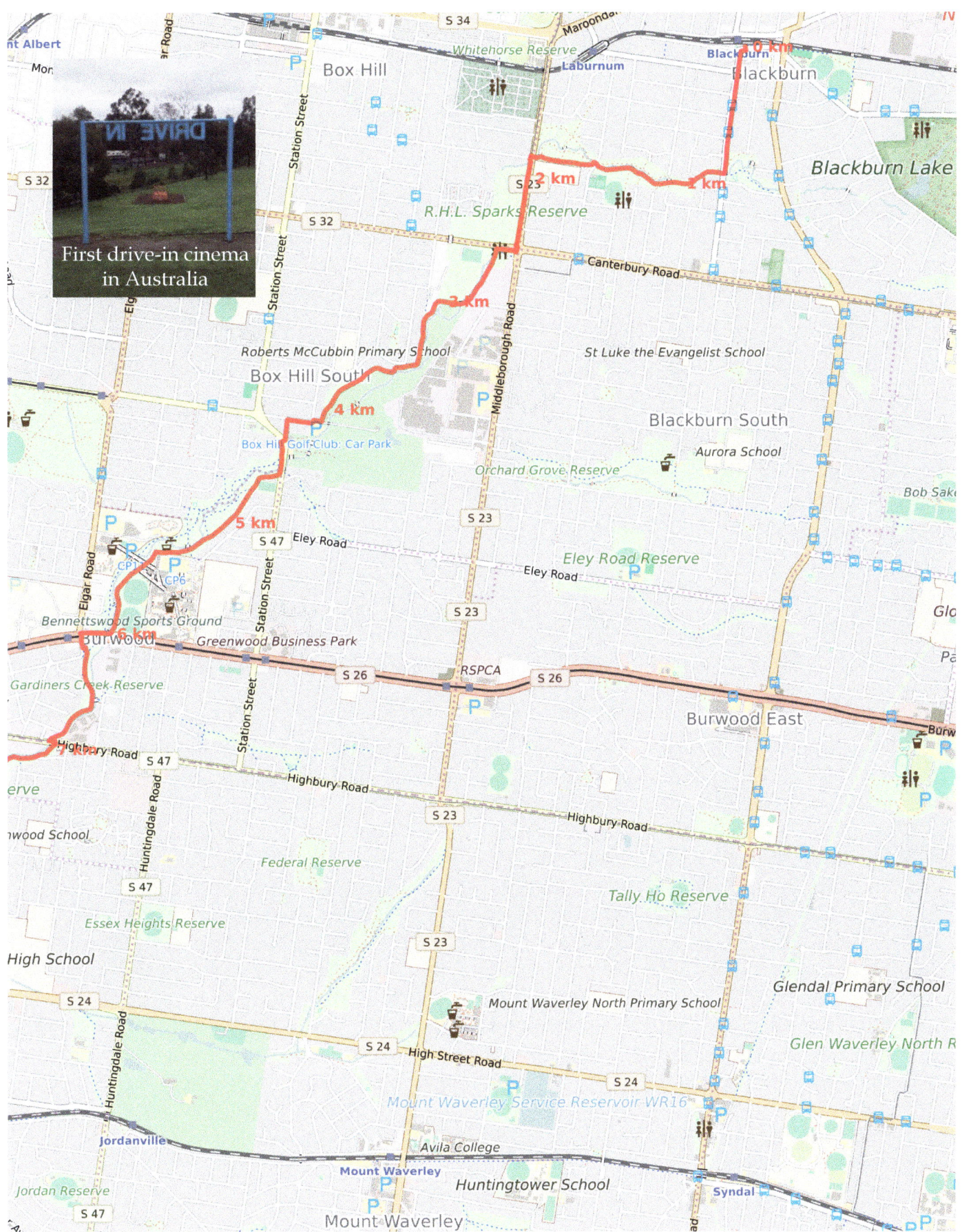

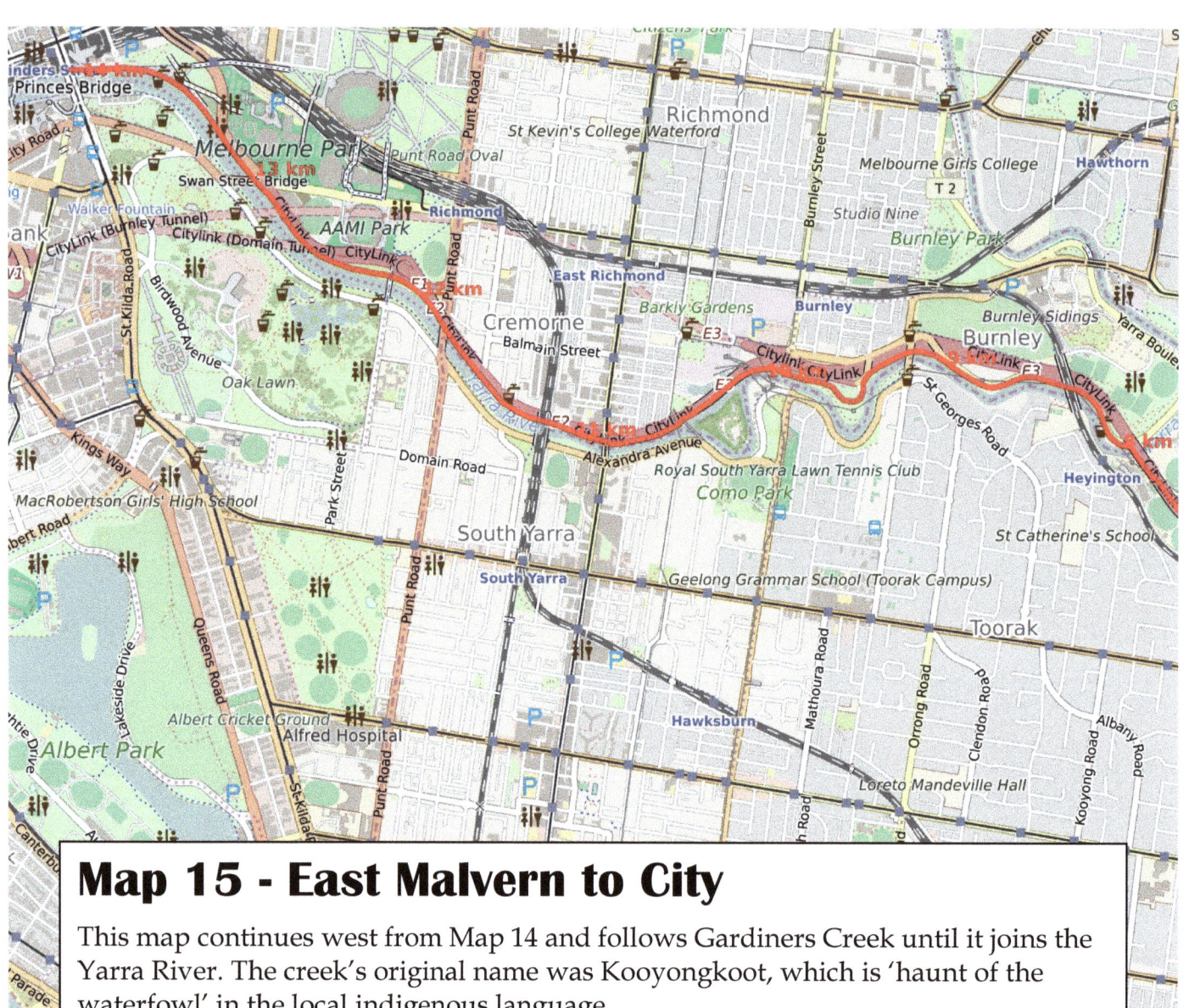

Map 15 - East Malvern to City

This map continues west from Map 14 and follows Gardiners Creek until it joins the Yarra River. The creek's original name was Kooyongkoot, which is 'haunt of the waterfowl' in the local indigenous language.

Distance: 14.0 km one-way (28.0 km return)

Elevation: 1 to 32 metres above sea level. Peak elevation is at the start.

Start point: East Malvern Station. **End point:** Federation Square

Be alert: Road crossings at Winton Rd (traffic lights), Dunlop St (traffic lights).

Try to spot: Kooyong Lawn Tennis Club, the original venue of the Australian Open.

Navigation tips: From East Malvern Station, take the overhead bridge over the Monash Freeway and walk across the golf course. Don't cross the footbridge over Gardiners Creek but go westwards along the Gardiners Creek Trail. At 6.7 km, the trail goes under the Monash Freeway, crossing the Creek at the same time. Keep heading west and you will find yourself walking along an elevated path attached to the underside of the Monash Freeway for a kilometre before crossing the Yarra River. Keep heading west, walking along the north bank of the Yarra River until you reach Federation Square.

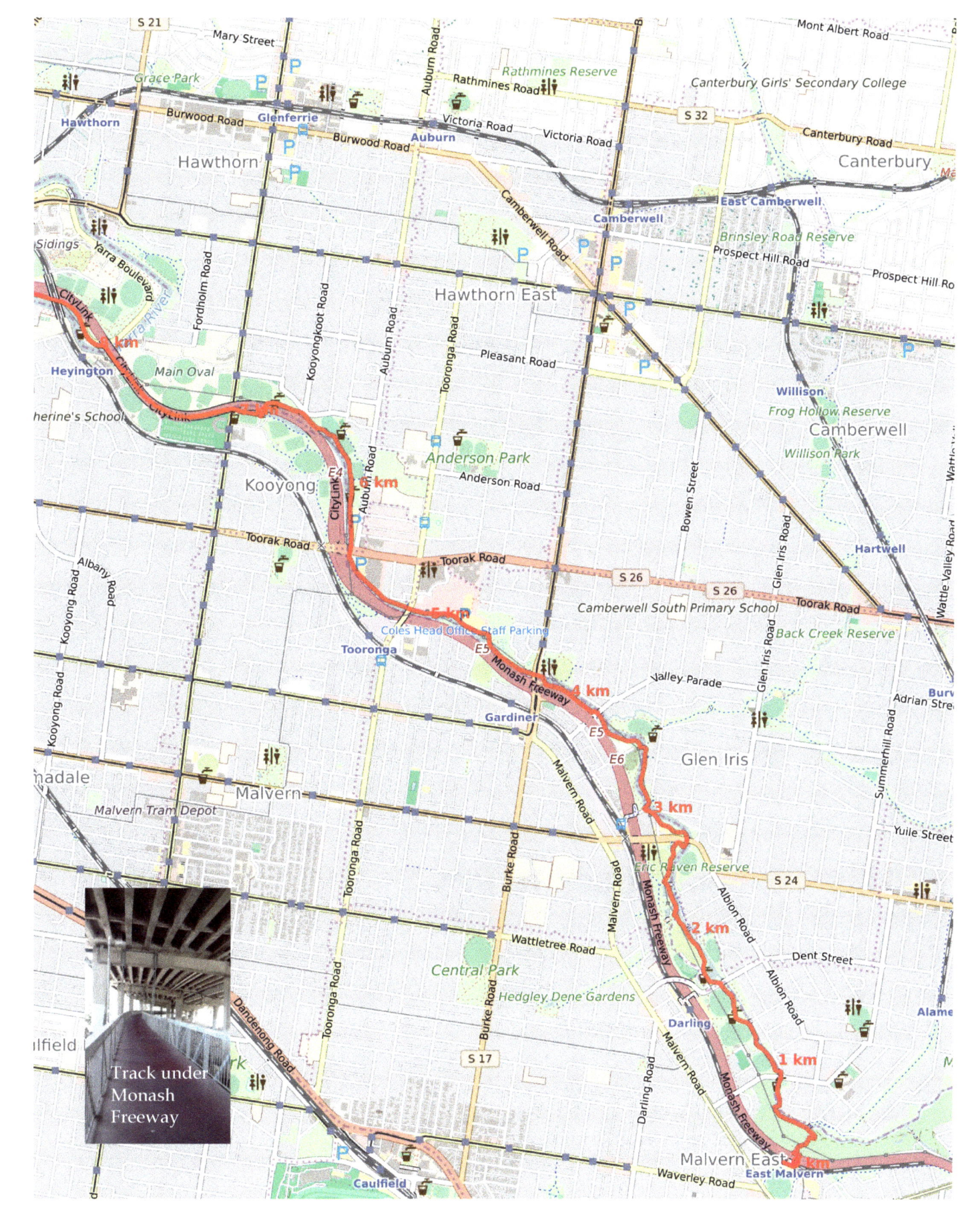
Track under Monash Freeway

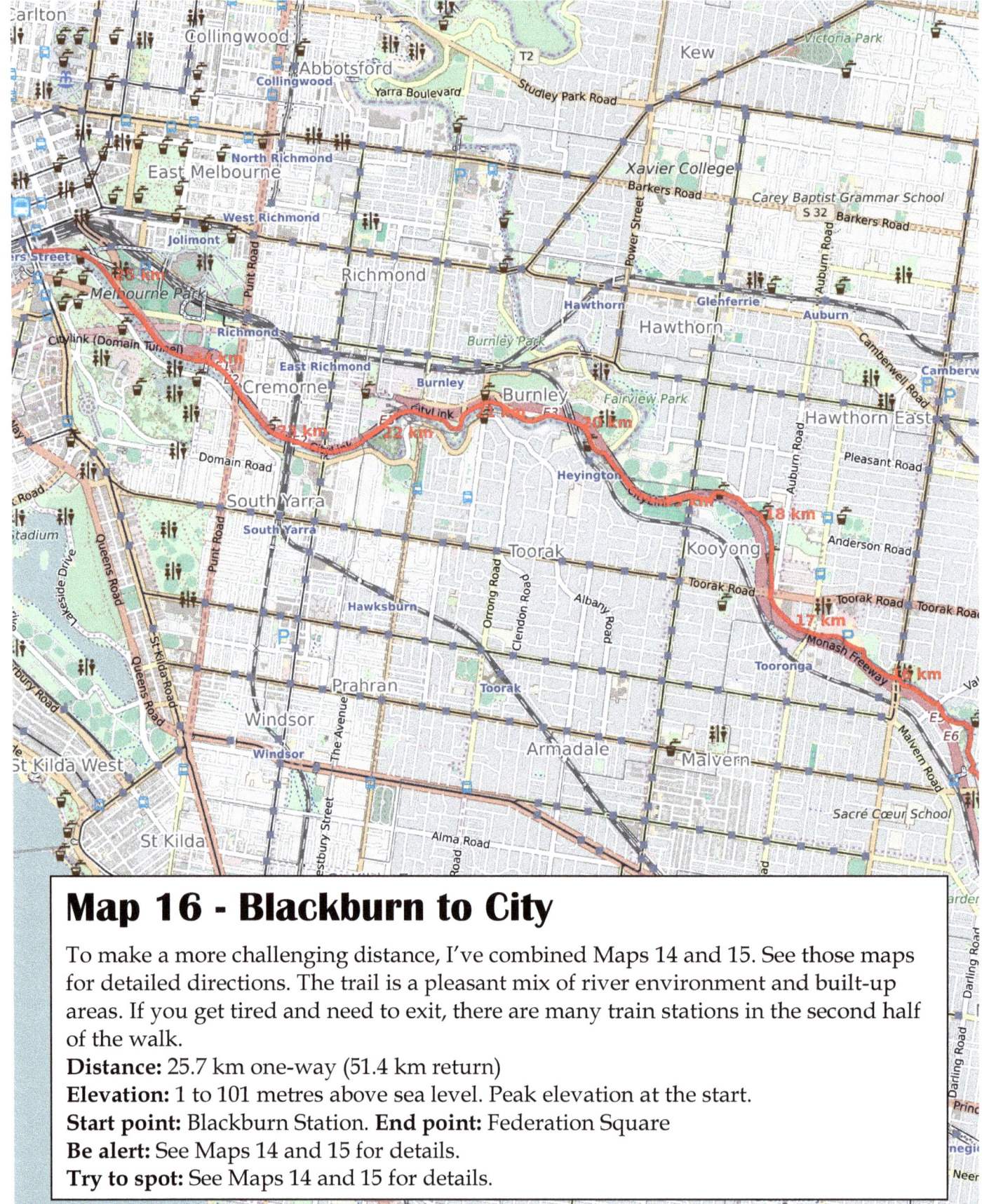

Map 16 - Blackburn to City

To make a more challenging distance, I've combined Maps 14 and 15. See those maps for detailed directions. The trail is a pleasant mix of river environment and built-up areas. If you get tired and need to exit, there are many train stations in the second half of the walk.

Distance: 25.7 km one-way (51.4 km return)

Elevation: 1 to 101 metres above sea level. Peak elevation at the start.

Start point: Blackburn Station. **End point:** Federation Square

Be alert: See Maps 14 and 15 for details.

Try to spot: See Maps 14 and 15 for details.

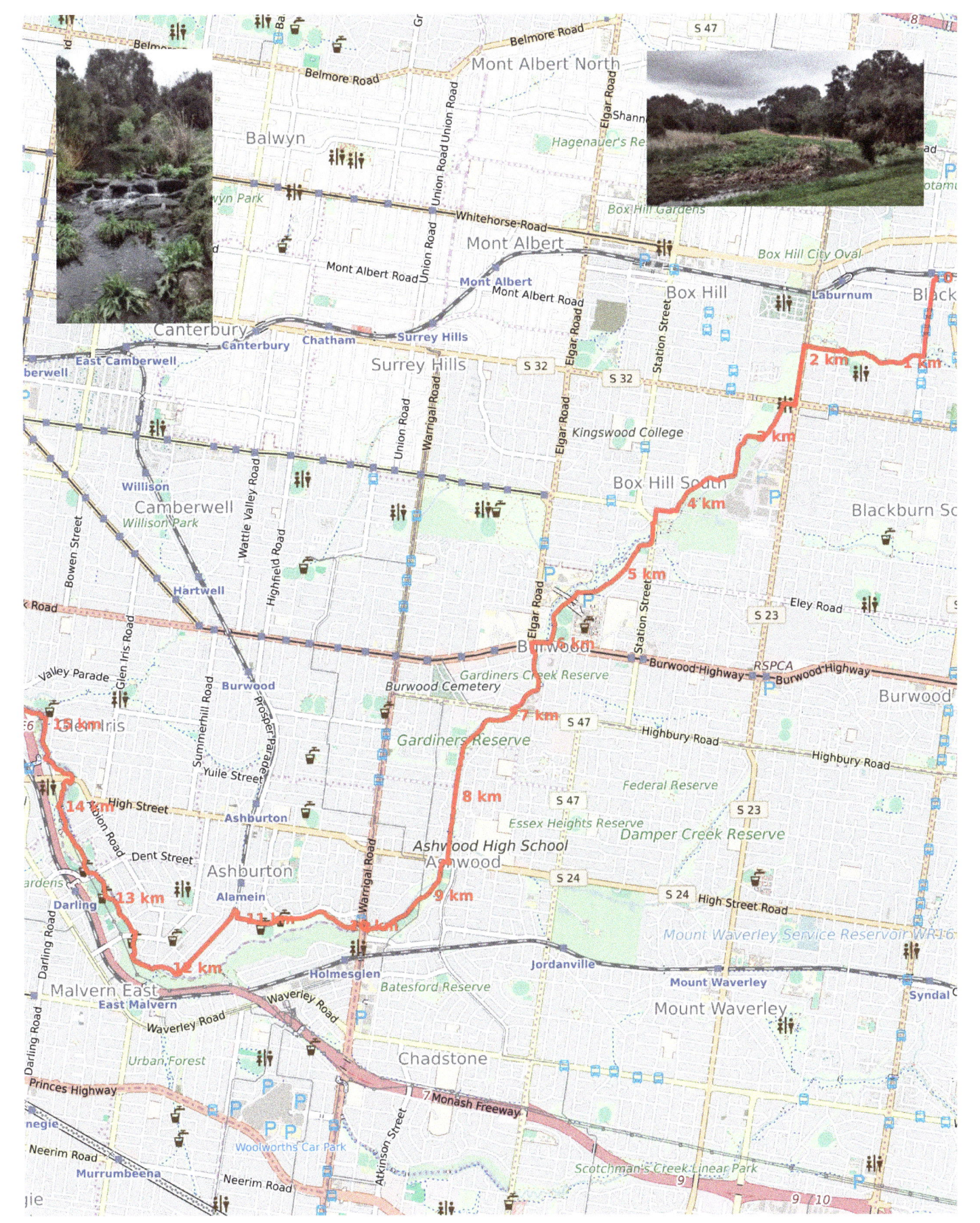

Map 17 - City to Fairfield Boathouse

This is one of my favourite river walks. It is a perfect mix of urban and natural landscapes.
Distance: 15.4 km one-way (30.8 km return)
Elevation: 1 to 35 metres above sea level. Peak elevation is at the end point.
Start point: Federation Square. **End point:** Fairfield Boathouse (500m from Dennis Station)
Be alert: Road crossing at Yarra Bend Rd.
Try to spot: A micro vineyard, Collingwood Farm, the Skipping Girl neon sign.
Navigation tips: Walk on the north bank of the Yarra River. Follow the Main Yarra Trail. At 10.0 km, cross the footbridge. At 10.6 km, go left (west) when you reach Yarra Boulevard. At 11.2 km, leave Yarra Boulevard and take the left fork. At 11.4 km, cross the footbridge, go down the stairs and walk north along the Yarra. At 13.6 km, cross the footbridge over Merri Creek then turn left. At 14.9 km, turn right and cross Yarra Bend Rd.

This map shows a magnified portion of the map on the right.

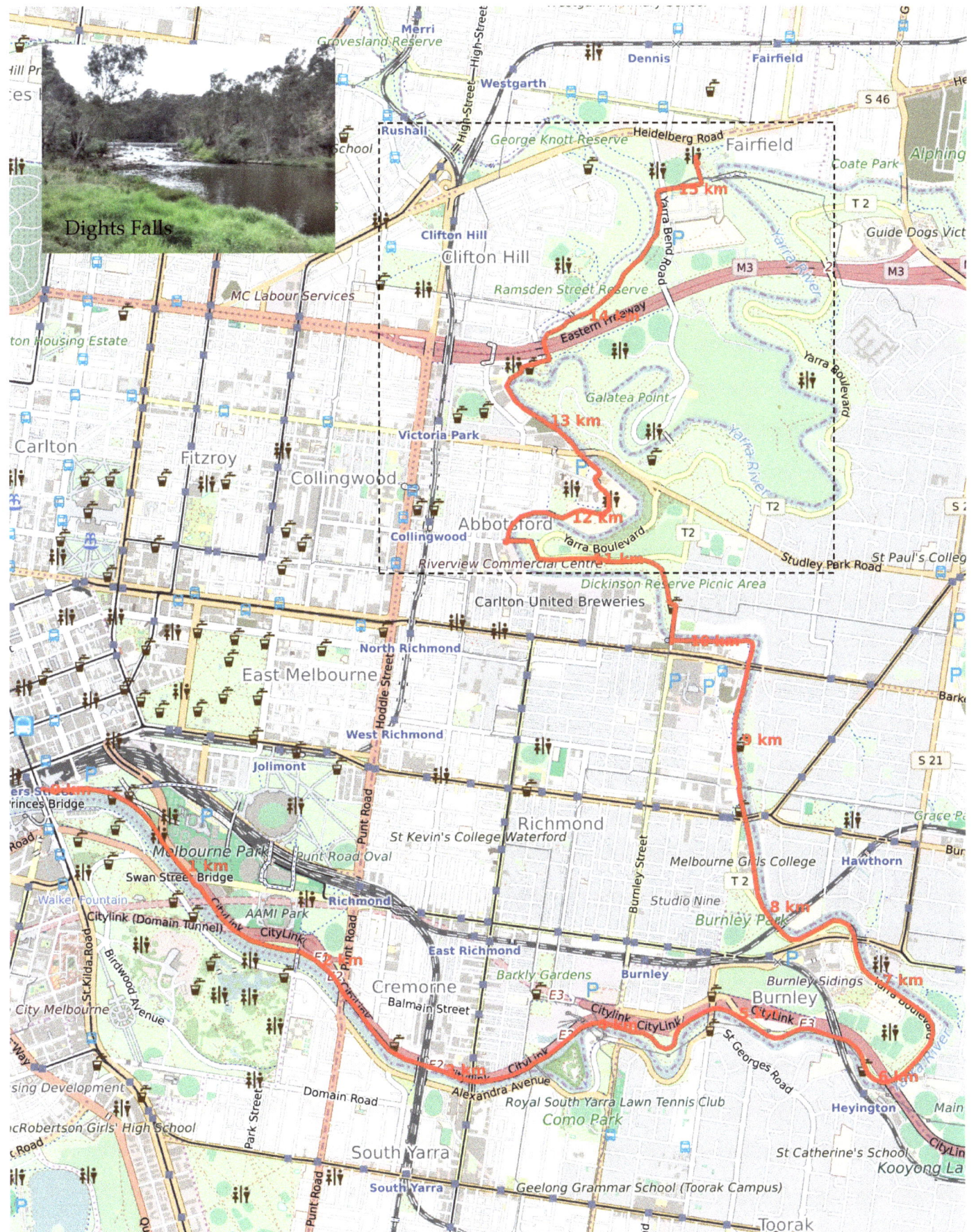

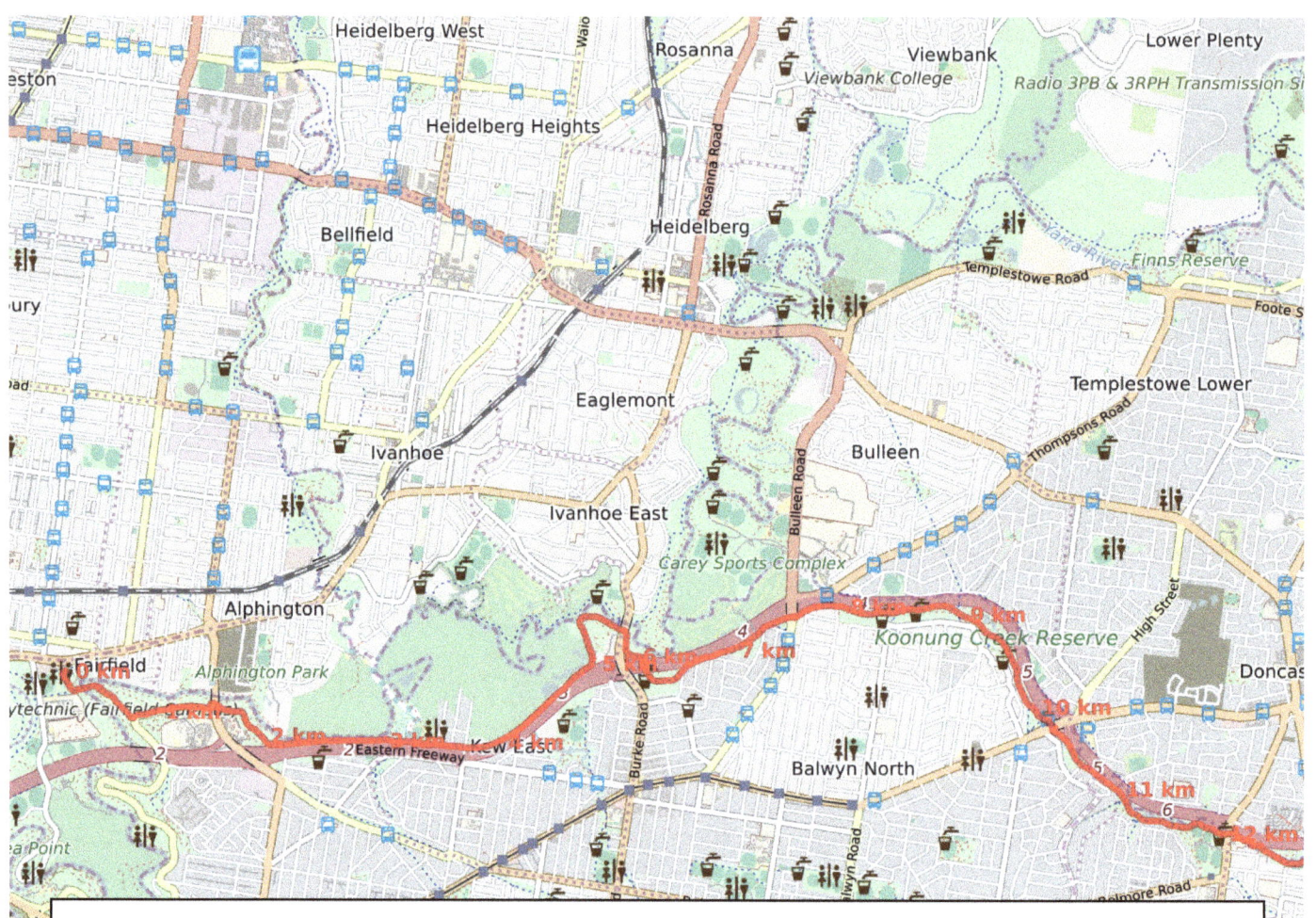

Map 18 - Fairfield to Ringwood

This trail uses the Main Yarra Trail, Koonung Creek Trail, the Eastlink Trail and finally the Mullum Mullum Creek Trail. It follows the Eastern Freeway closely.

Distance: 24.2 km one-way (48.4 km return)

Elevation: 6 to 128 metres above sea level. Peak elevation is at the 18.5 km mark.

Start point: Fairfield Boathouse (about 500 metres from Dennis Station)

End point: Ringwood Station

Be alert: Road crossings at Belford Rd, Bulleen Rd (traffic lights), Doncaster Rd (traffic lights), Elgar Rd (traffic lights), Maroondah Highway (traffic lights).

Try to spot: Wurundjeri Spur Lookout, Kew Billabong, Schwerkolt Cottage

Navigation tips: Starting from the carpark near Fairfield Boathouse, follow the Main Yarra Trail down the slope. Cross the pipe bridge and climb up to Yarra Boulevard. Turn left (eastwards) and at 1.4 km go down the stairs to go under Chandler Highway. At 5.7 km, start following the Koonung Creek Trail. At 13.6 km, you will be crossing over the Eastern Freeway. At 17.7 km, the trail becomes the Eastlink Trail. At 22.5 km, leave the Eastlink Trail and follow the Mullum Mullum Creek Trail. At 23.4 km, leave the trail and walk south along Ringwood St. In 600 metres, you will reach Ringwood Station.

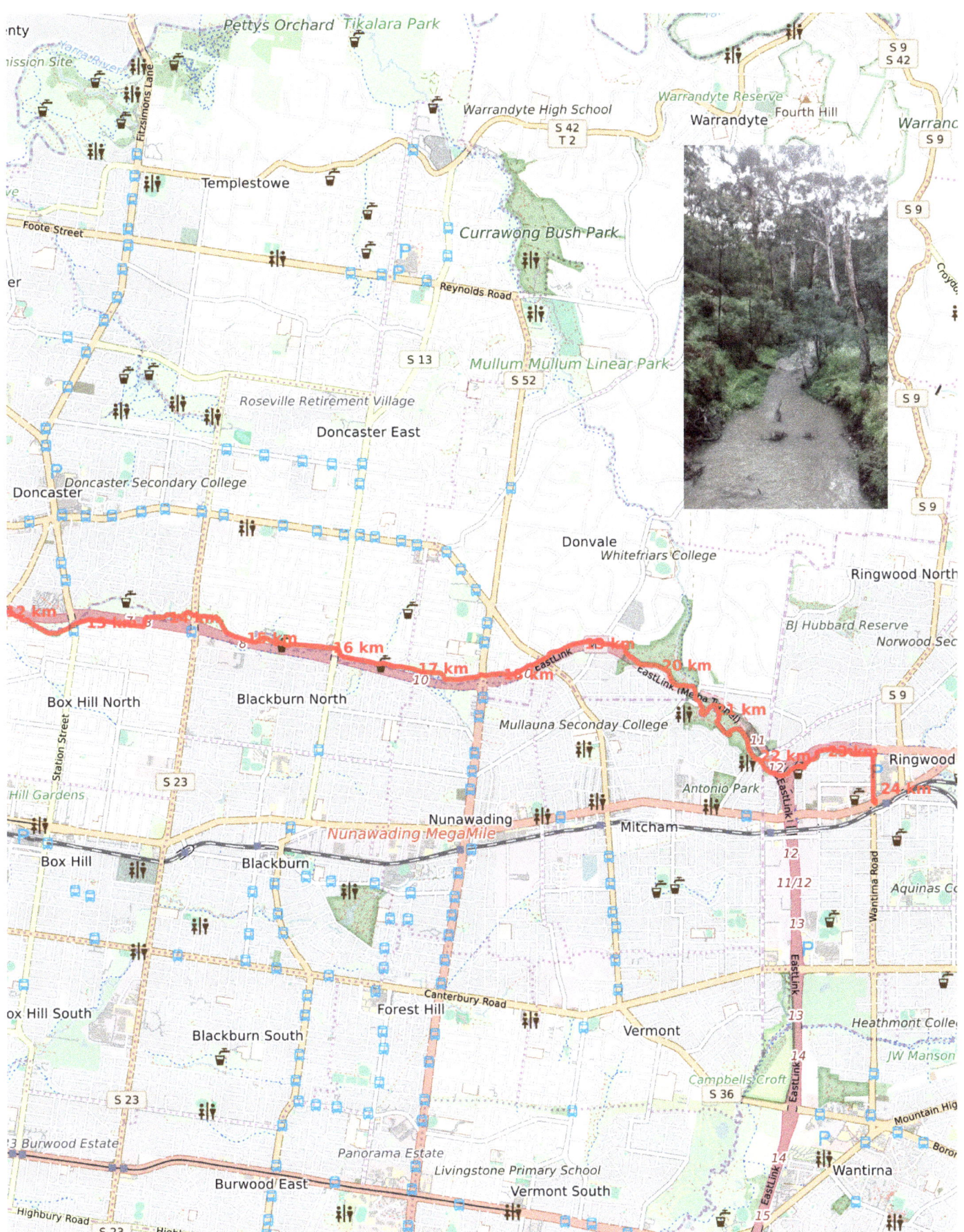

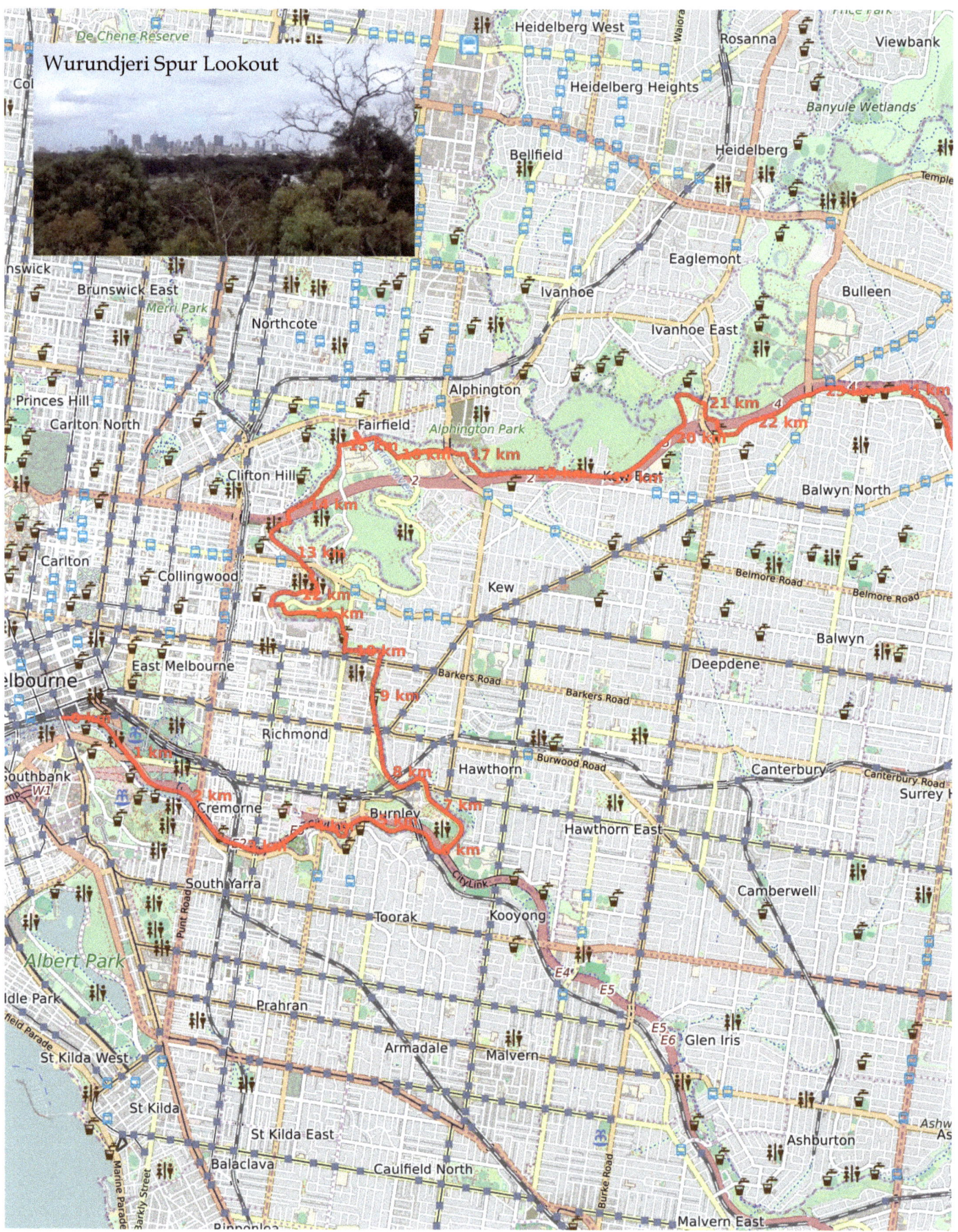

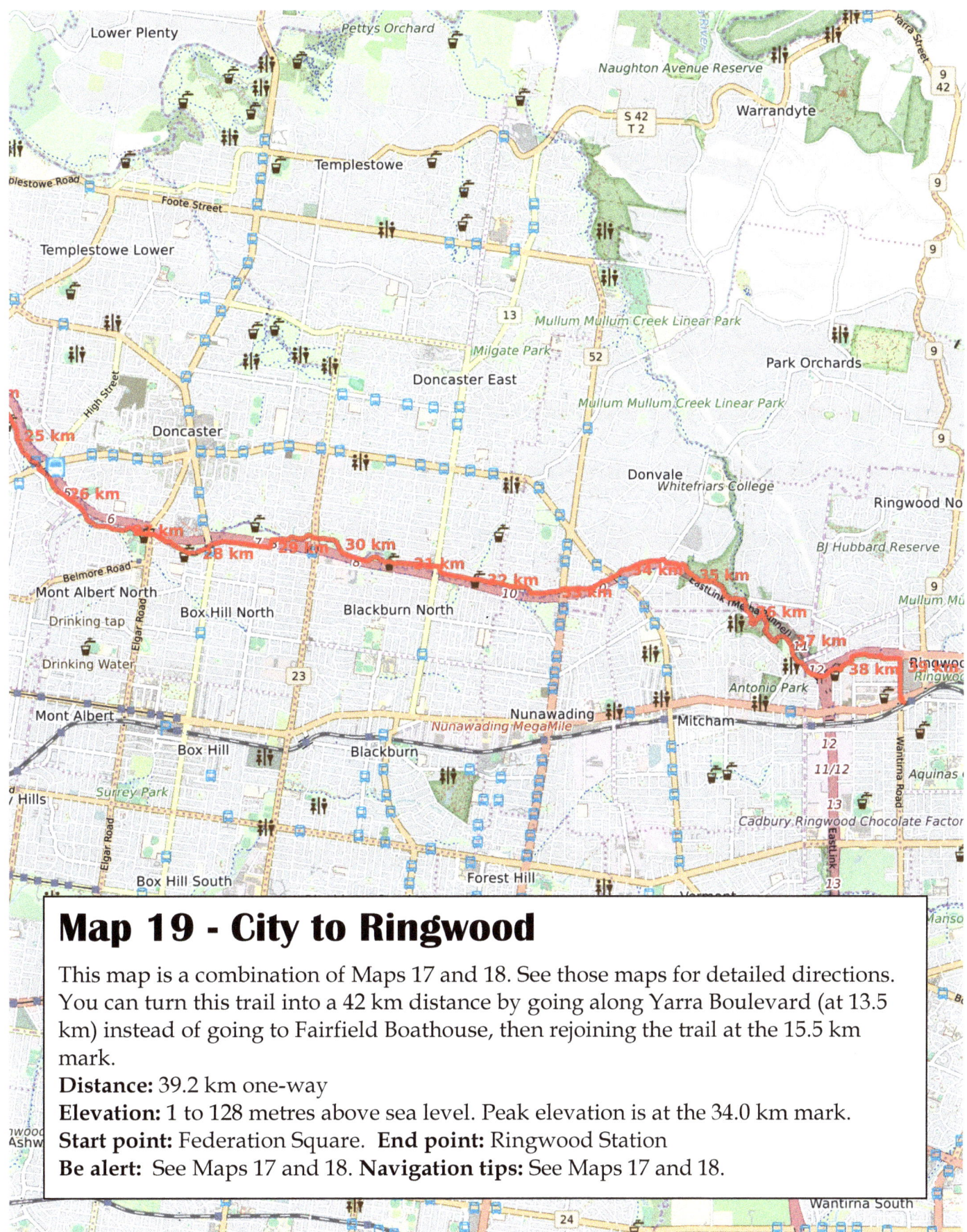

Map 19 - City to Ringwood

This map is a combination of Maps 17 and 18. See those maps for detailed directions. You can turn this trail into a 42 km distance by going along Yarra Boulevard (at 13.5 km) instead of going to Fairfield Boathouse, then rejoining the trail at the 15.5 km mark.

Distance: 39.2 km one-way

Elevation: 1 to 128 metres above sea level. Peak elevation is at the 34.0 km mark.

Start point: Federation Square. **End point:** Ringwood Station

Be alert: See Maps 17 and 18. **Navigation tips:** See Maps 17 and 18.

Map 20 - The Thousand Steps

This trail commemorates the battle for the Kokoda Track in Papua New Guinea during World War II. By the way, there are only 776 steps, not 1000 ☺. If the steps are busy, you can take the Lyrebird Track which is parallel to the steps. Take a break at the top with a picnic. To go back down, I suggest taking the Belview Terrace track which is longer but flatter and more peaceful.

Distance: 7.0 km circuit
Elevation: 123 to 513 metres above sea level.
Start and end points: Upper Ferntree Gully Station
Be alert: Runners sprinting up and down the narrow steps
Try to spot: The various signboards describing battle for the Kokoda Track.
Navigation tips: Start at the north side of Upper Ferntree Gully Station. Follow the cycling path. Walk through the car park and you will soon see the starting arch of the steps. At 1.5 km, you will start climbing the steps. At 2.8 km, the steps end. Walk forward, cross Lord Somers Road to the picnic grounds and have a break. (public toilets there). Turnaround and when you reach Lord Somers Road again, take the right fork (Ramu Ave). Head downwards and find Belview Terrace track and before long you will be back at the entrance of the car park. It's a short distance to Upper Ferntree Gully Station.

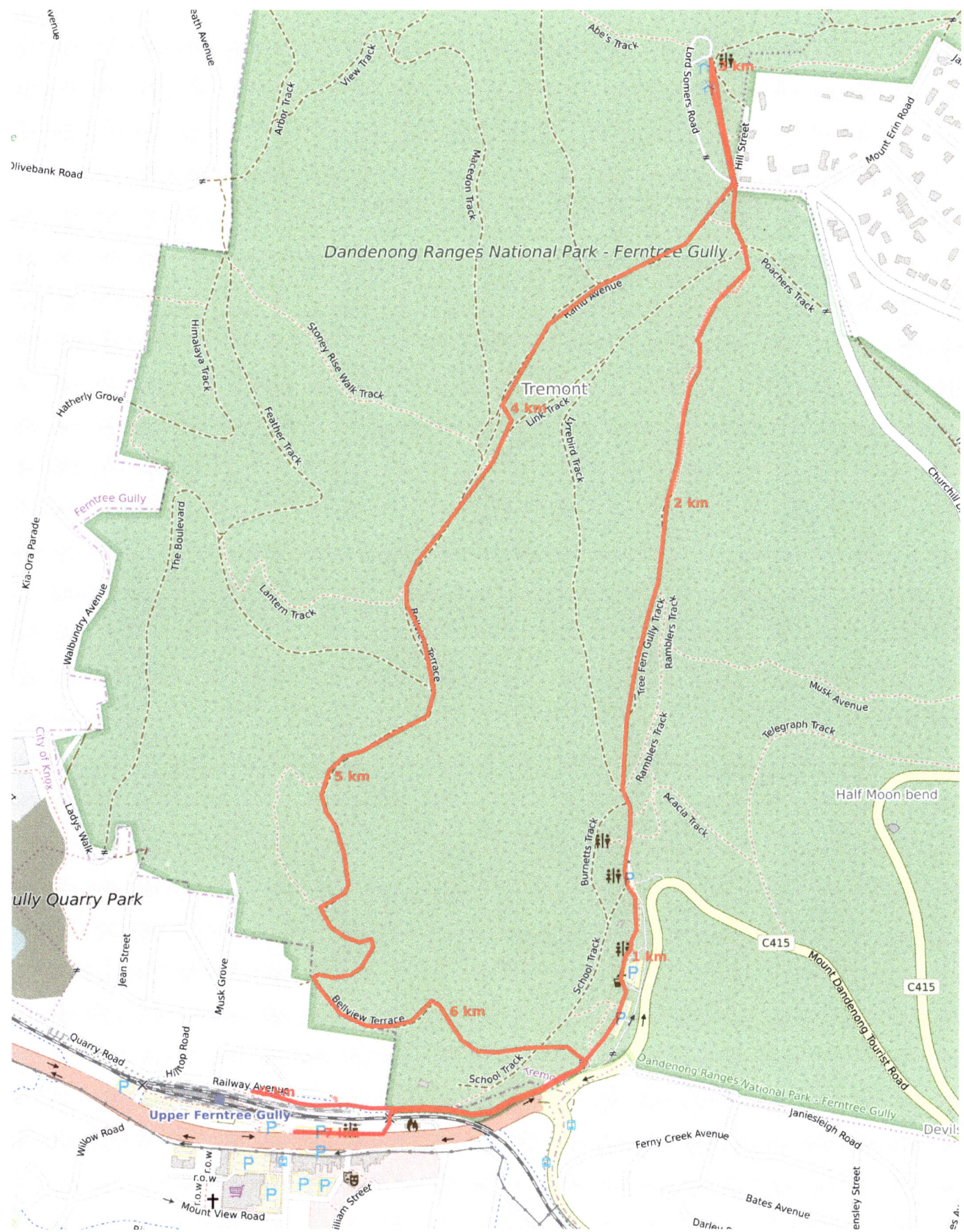

Map 21 - City to Station Pier (and back)

When Station Pier opened in 1854, it was linked via railway to Flinders Street Station. In 1987, the railway line closed. This walk parallels an old railway line and is called the Sandridge Trail.

Distance: 9.8 km return.

Elevation: 1 to 11 metres above sea level. Peak elevation is at the start.

Start and end points: Federation Square

Be alert: Road crossings at Queensbridge St (traffic lights), Clarendon St (traffic lights), Normanby Rd (traffic lights), tram track crossing near the tram depot, Ingles St, Bridge St, Swallow St (traffic lights), Beach St (traffic lights), Waterfront Place

Try to spot: Melbourne Convention & Exhibition Centre, tram depot, Station Pier

Navigation tips: From Federation Square, walk down Princes Bridge and get onto Southbank. Walk up to the Melbourne Convention & Exhibition Centre and turn left. Cross Normanby Rd and start walking beside the tram line. The tram line goes all the way to Station Pier. When you reach the last tram stop, walk eastwards for a short distance and you will find a little jetty with great views of the bay and St Kilda. Retrace your steps to get back to the start.

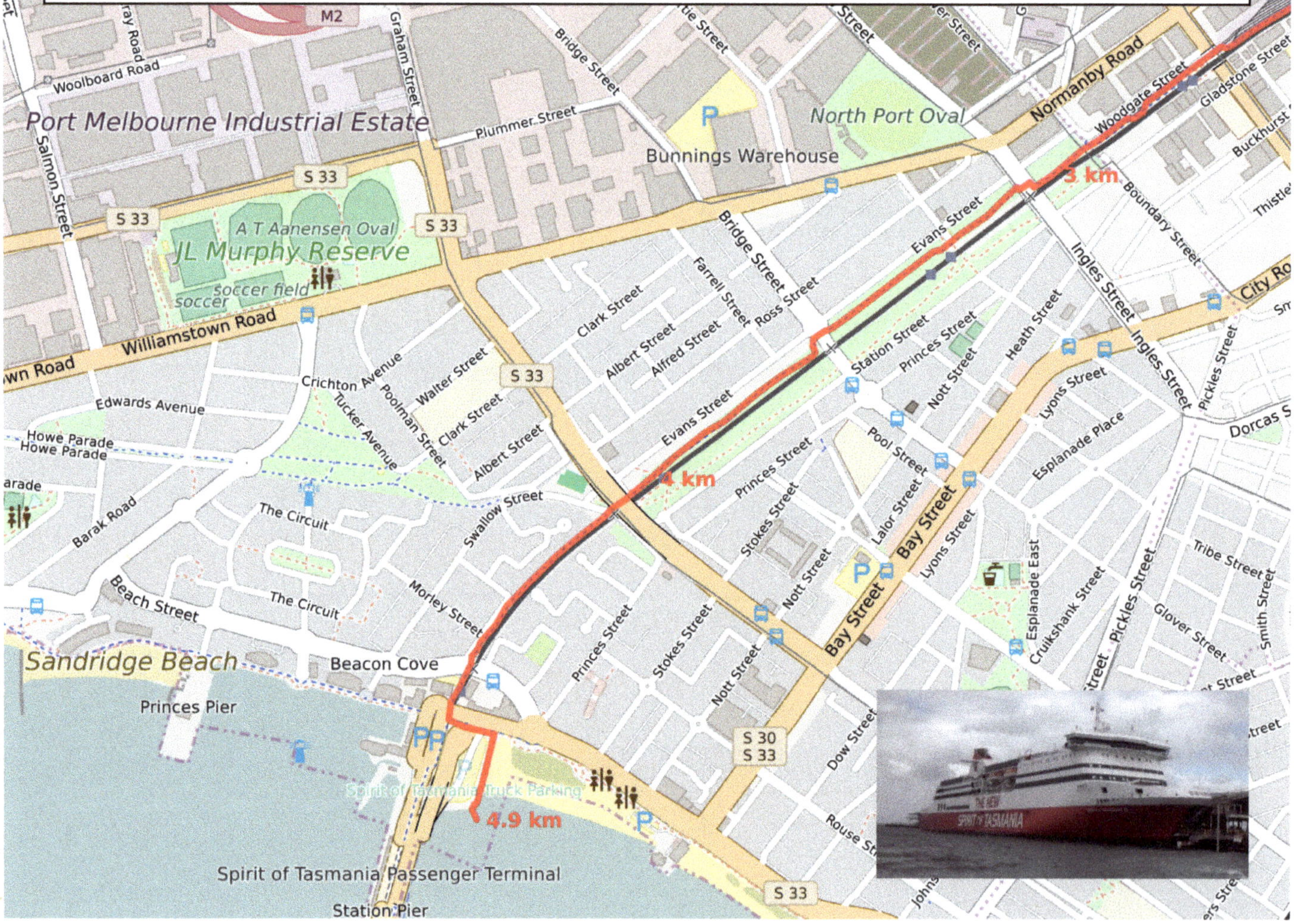

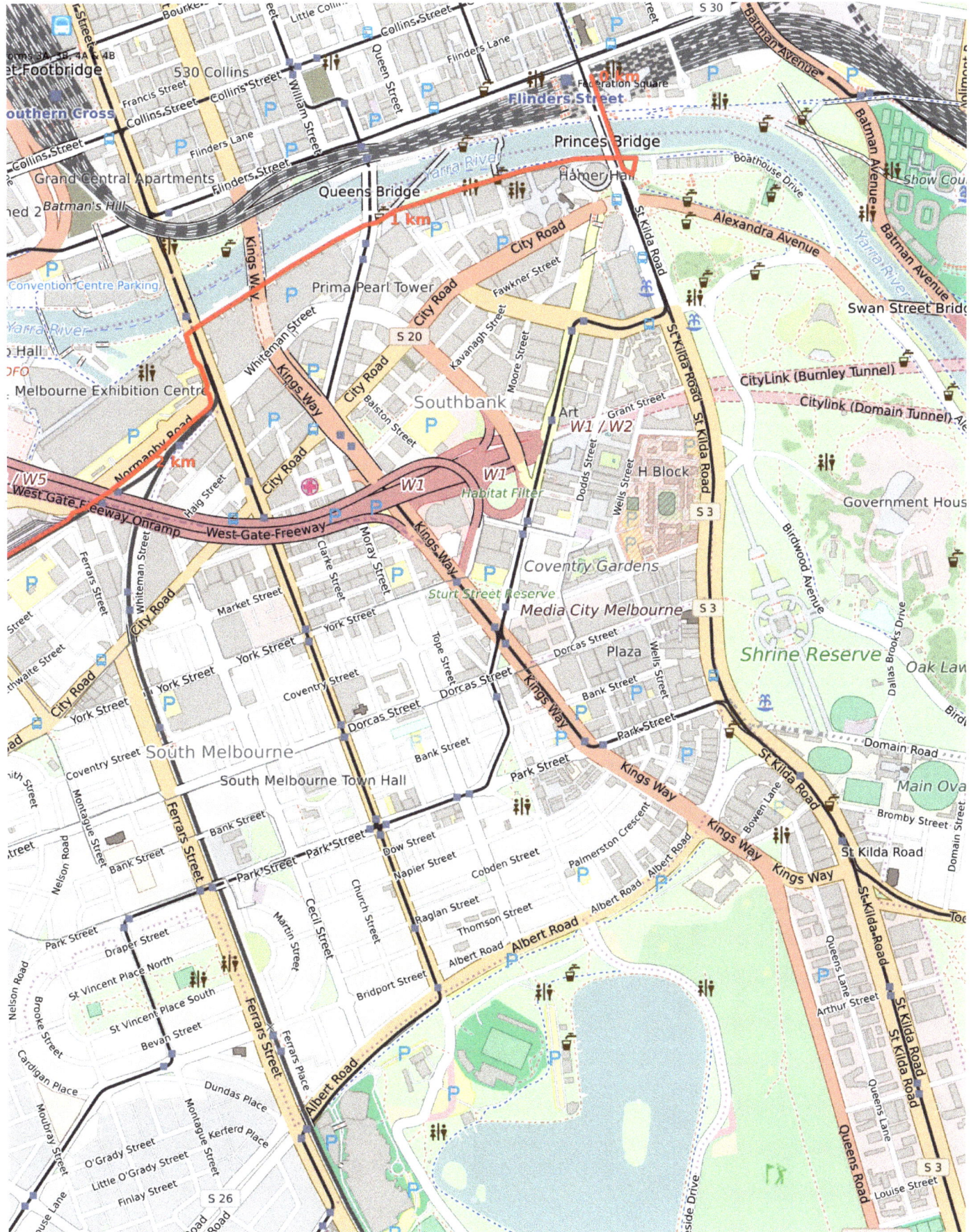

Map 22 - City to St Kilda

Melbourne's first Governor, Charles La Trobe, named St Kilda after the ship 'Lady of St Kilda', which moored in Melbourne in the 1840s. On this trail, you will encounter several Melbourne landmarks such as the Shrine of Remembrance and Albert Park Lake.

Distance: 8.6 km one-way.
Elevation: 1 to 31 metres above sea level. Peak elevation is at 1.4 km (The Shrine).
Start point: Federation Square.   **End point:** Luna Park, St Kilda
Be alert: Road crossings at Southbank Blvd (traffic lights), Government House Dr, Anzac Ave, St Kilda Rd (traffic lights), Albert Rd, Kings Way (traffic lights), Lakeside Dr (traffic lights), Albert Rd Dr, Ross Gregory Dr, Village Green Dr, Balluk William Ct, Canterbury Rd (traffic lights), Loch St, Park Ln, Park St (traffic lights), Beaconsfield Pde (traffic lights), Jacka Blvd (traffic lights), Pier Rd, Marine Pde (traffic lights).
Try to spot: Shrine of Remembrance, Albert Park, St Kilda Pier, Palais Theatre, Luna Park
Navigation tips: From Federation Square head to the Shrine of Remembrance. Cross two busy roads, St Kilda Rd and Kings Way, to get to Albert Park Lake. You can go clockwise or anticlockwise around the lake, both ways are equally scenic. When you reach the southernmost tip of the lake (at 5.0 km), leave the lake via a footpath and follow footpaths to Fitzroy St. When you reach Catani Gardens, head to St Kilda Pier for a coffee stop at the end of the pier. You can watch penguins at this pier if you happen to go at sunset. Go back to the beach and head south until you see Luna Park. You can go to cafes here and take trams back to the city.

Map 23 - St Kilda to South Melbourne Market

South Melbourne Market began in 1867 and is Melbourne's oldest continually-running market. This walk follows the beach and then the Sandridge Trail before turning off to the market. **Distance:** 8.7 km one-way.

Elevation: 1 to 11 metres above sea level. Peak elevation is at the end.

Start point: Luna Park, St Kilda (trams 3, 16 and 96)

End point: South Melbourne Market (trams 96 and 12).

Be alert: Road crossings at Marine Pde (traffic lights), Station Pier's industrial entrance, Waterfront Pl, Beach St (traffic lights), Swallow St (traffic lights), Bridge St, Ingles St, tram track crossing near the tram depot, Meaden St, City Rd (traffic lights), Market St, York St.

Try to spot: St Kilda Pier, Station Pier, a tram depot

Navigation tips: From Luna Park, go to the beach and head west. At 5.4 km, you will reach Station Pier. Turn right and head north-east, following the Sandridge Trail. After you pass the tram depot, there is a tram stop ahead (at the 7.8 km mark). Leave the trail by crossing the tram tracks and walk along Meaden St. When you reach City Rd, cross at the traffic lights nearby and walk along Market St. When you hit a roundabout, turn right and walk down Cecil St all the way to the market.

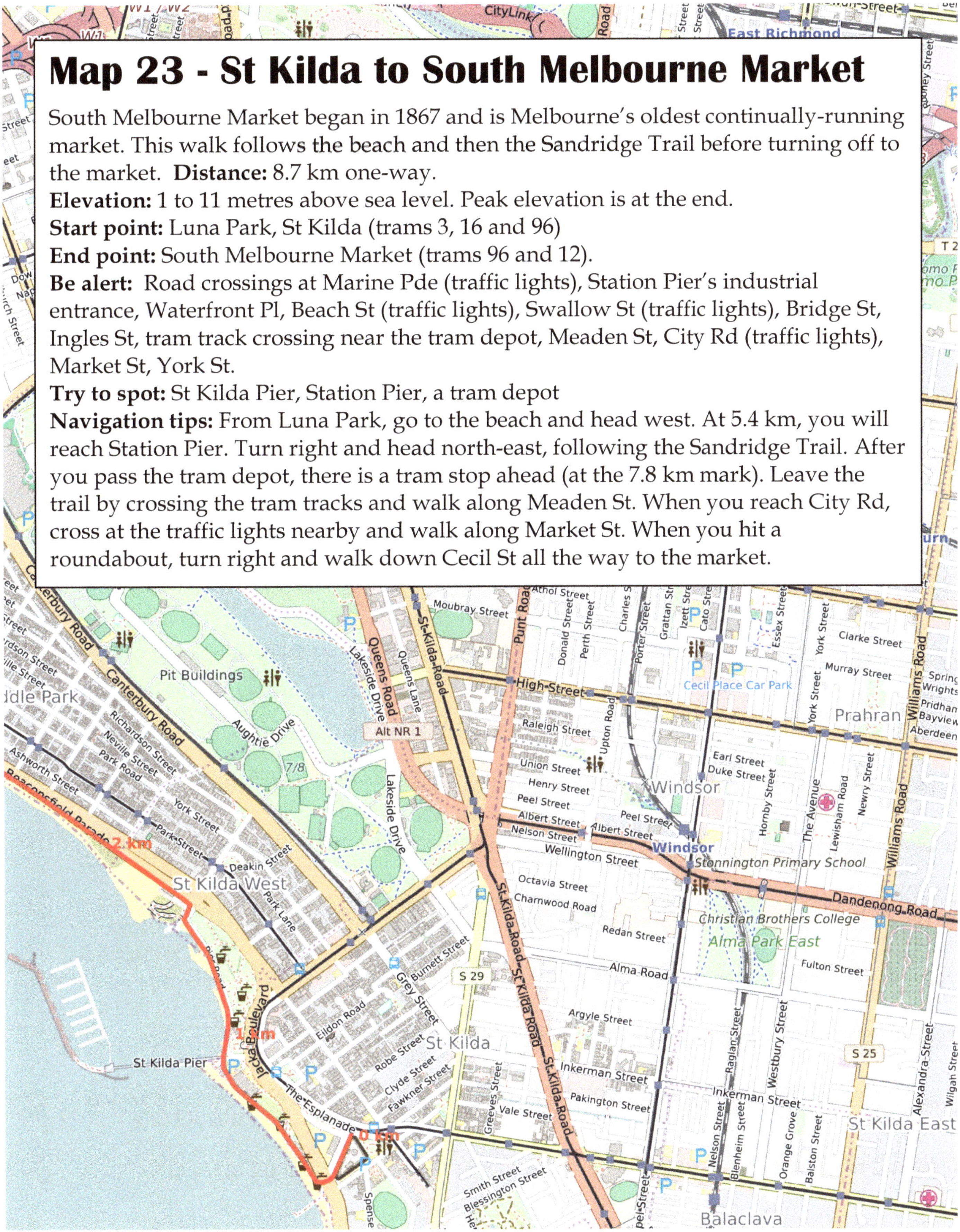

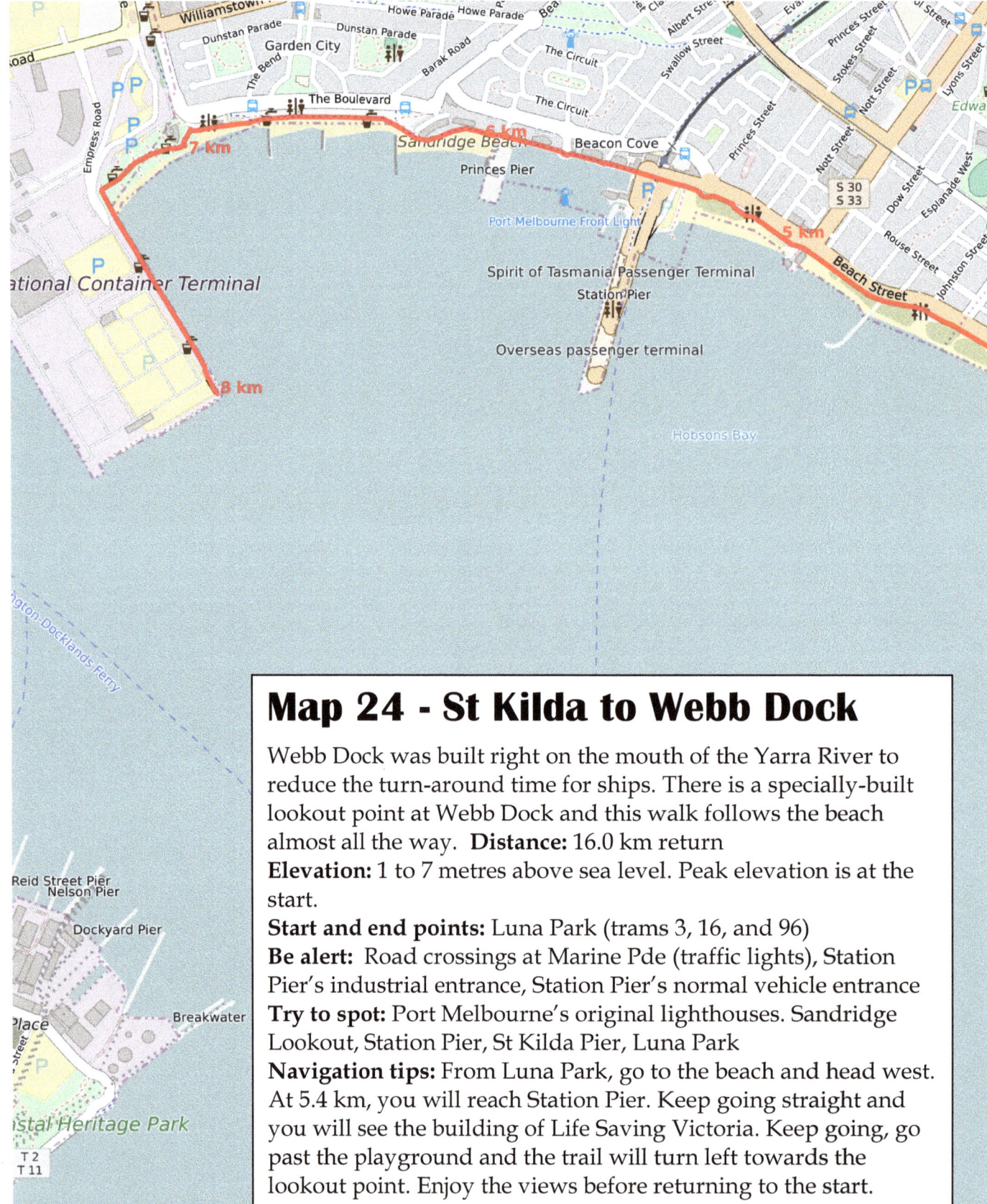

Map 24 - St Kilda to Webb Dock

Webb Dock was built right on the mouth of the Yarra River to reduce the turn-around time for ships. There is a specially-built lookout point at Webb Dock and this walk follows the beach almost all the way. **Distance:** 16.0 km return

Elevation: 1 to 7 metres above sea level. Peak elevation is at the start.

Start and end points: Luna Park (trams 3, 16, and 96)

Be alert: Road crossings at Marine Pde (traffic lights), Station Pier's industrial entrance, Station Pier's normal vehicle entrance

Try to spot: Port Melbourne's original lighthouses. Sandridge Lookout, Station Pier, St Kilda Pier, Luna Park

Navigation tips: From Luna Park, go to the beach and head west. At 5.4 km, you will reach Station Pier. Keep going straight and you will see the building of Life Saving Victoria. Keep going, go past the playground and the trail will turn left towards the lookout point. Enjoy the views before returning to the start.

Sandridge Lookout

'Pink Lake'

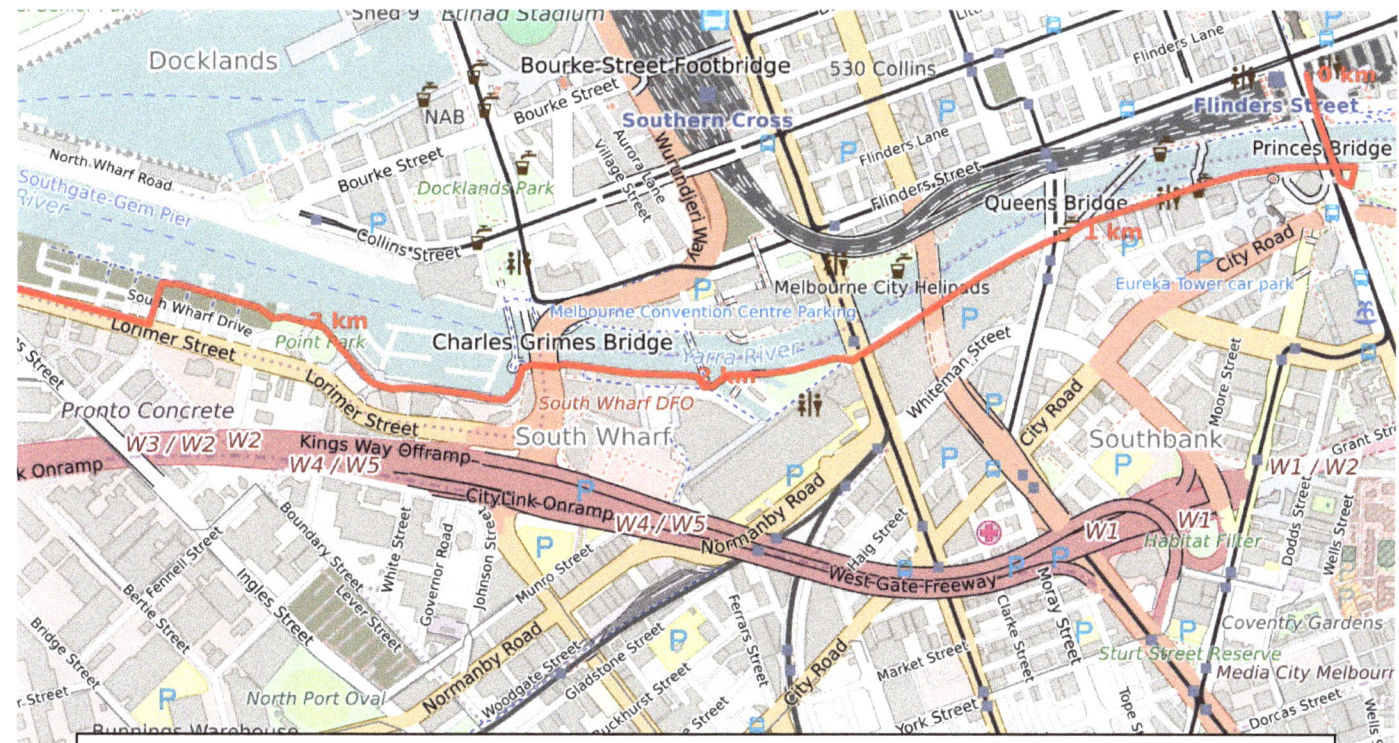

Map 25 – Fishermans Bend

From the 1850s, the area was occupied by fishermen, hence the name. The last remaining fisherman shack was demolished in 1970. This walk probably has the most varied scenery in the book, going through the cityscape, then industrial areas, followed by Westgate Park and finally the beach.

Distance: 13.5 km one-way or 11.3 km if you skip the leg to the lookout.

Elevation: 1 to 10 metres above sea level. Peak elevation is at the start.

Start point: Federation Square

End point: Station Pier (near tram 109).

Be alert: Road crossings at Queensbridge St (traffic lights), Clarendon St (traffic lights), South Wharf Dr, Lorimer St, Ingles St, Hall St, Salmon St (traffic lights), Inner Ring Rd, Westside Ave, Bayside Ave, Lorimer St (again), Todd Rd Detour (twice, with traffic lights), Williamstown Rd (traffic lights), Station Pier entrance

Try to spot: Bolte Bridge, Webb Dock Lookout (from afar), a pink lake at Westgate Park (only during warmer months)

Navigation tips: From Federation Square, get onto the south bank of the Yarra and keep walking until you get close to the Bolte Bridge. At this point go left and walk along Lorimer St. At 5.9 km, cross Todd Rd carefully (the crossing is at a bend in the road) and get onto another track. The track will bring you under the West Gate Bridge and through Westgate Park. Exit at the south-east corner of the park and walk south towards the beach. At 9.8 km, when you reach the beach, head west to the Webb Dock Lookout. Then retrace your steps to the beach and continue east to get to Station Pier.

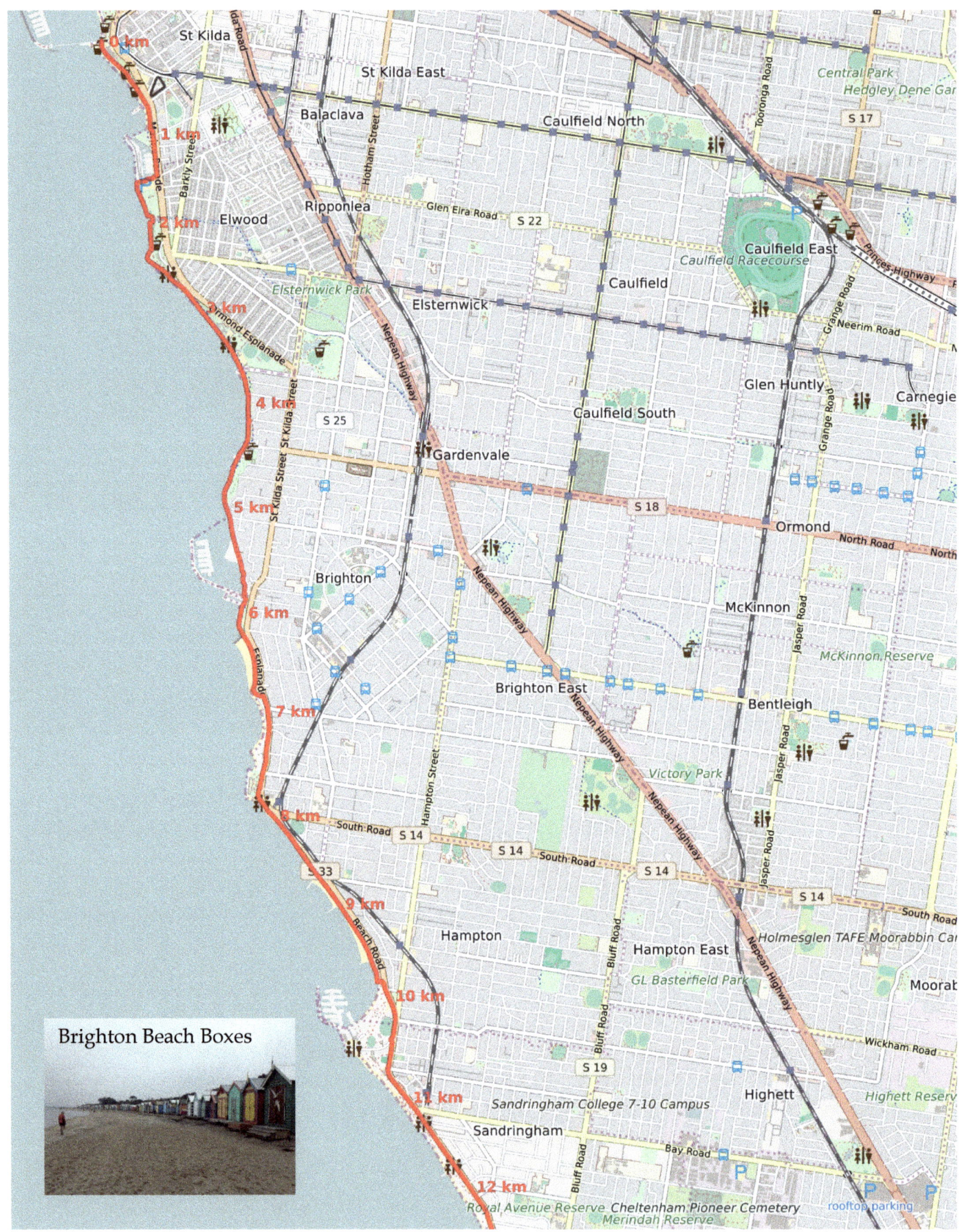

Brighton Beach Boxes

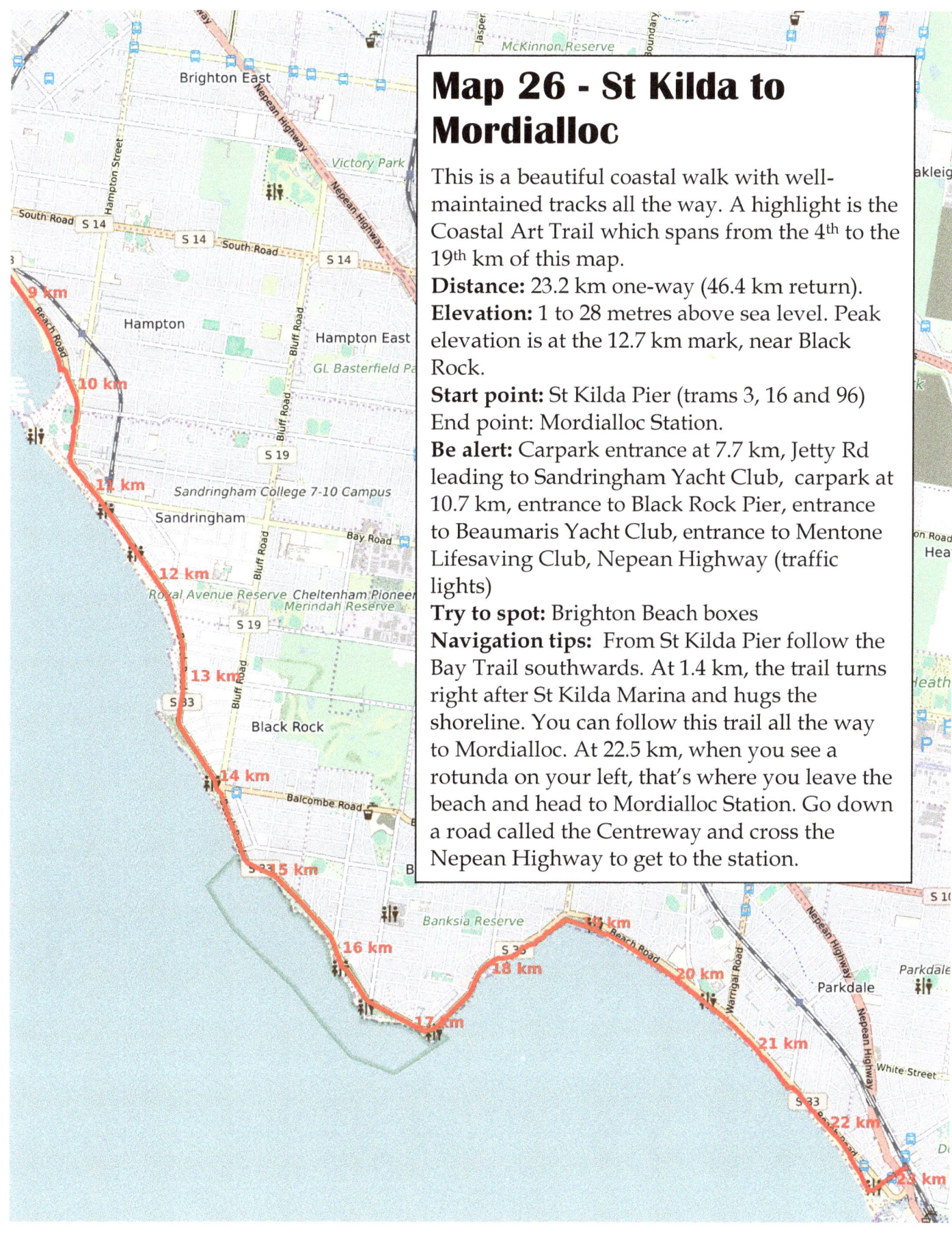

Map 26 - St Kilda to Mordialloc

This is a beautiful coastal walk with well-maintained tracks all the way. A highlight is the Coastal Art Trail which spans from the 4th to the 19th km of this map.

Distance: 23.2 km one-way (46.4 km return).

Elevation: 1 to 28 metres above sea level. Peak elevation is at the 12.7 km mark, near Black Rock.

Start point: St Kilda Pier (trams 3, 16 and 96)
End point: Mordialloc Station.

Be alert: Carpark entrance at 7.7 km, Jetty Rd leading to Sandringham Yacht Club, carpark at 10.7 km, entrance to Black Rock Pier, entrance to Beaumaris Yacht Club, entrance to Mentone Lifesaving Club, Nepean Highway (traffic lights)

Try to spot: Brighton Beach boxes

Navigation tips: From St Kilda Pier follow the Bay Trail southwards. At 1.4 km, the trail turns right after St Kilda Marina and hugs the shoreline. You can follow this trail all the way to Mordialloc. At 22.5 km, when you see a rotunda on your left, that's where you leave the beach and head to Mordialloc Station. Go down a road called the Centreway and cross the Nepean Highway to get to the station.

Patterson Lakes

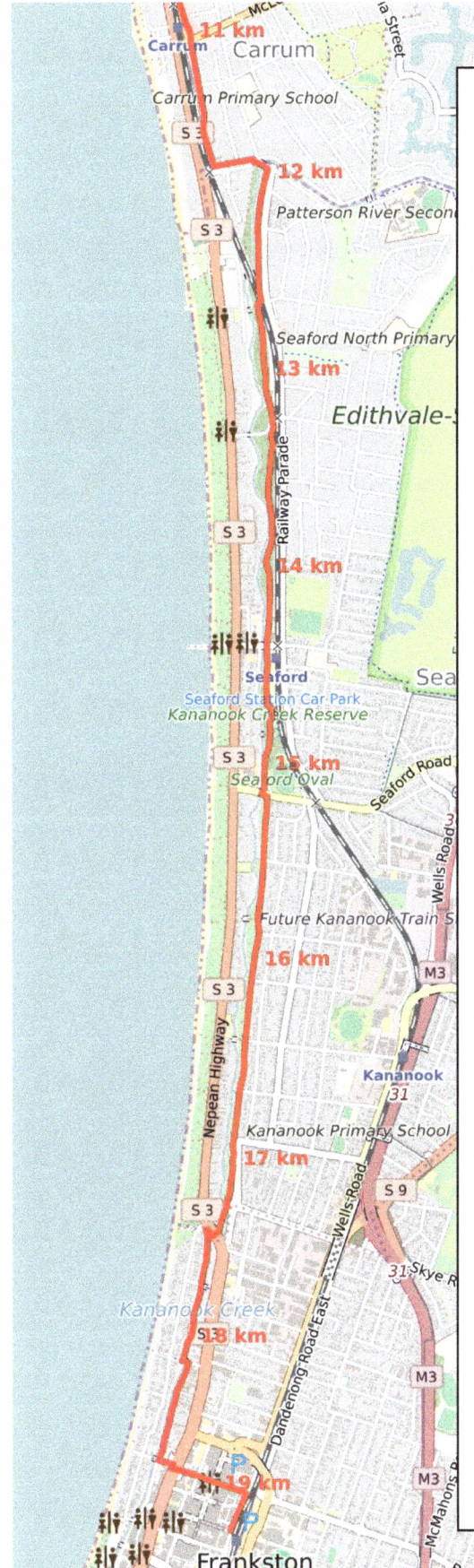

Map 27 - Mordialloc to Frankston

This track goes inland for the first half along the Long Beach Trail and after crossing Patterson River, head for the Kannanook Creek Trail.

Distance: 19.3 km one-way (38.6 km return)
Elevation: 1 to 10 metres above sea level. Peak elevation is at the 12.8 km mark.
Start point: Mordialloc Station
End point: Frankston Station
Be alert: Road crossings at Bear St, Edithvale Rd (traffic lights), Thames Promenade (traffic lights), McLeod Rd (traffic lights), Walker Rd, Kalimna St, Eel Race Rd (traffic lights), crossing at Frankston railway tracks, Armstrongs Rd, McKenzie St, Seaford Rd, Nepean Highway, Beach St, Nepean Highway (again, this time with traffic lights), Olsen St, Young St (traffic lights)
Try to spot: Edithvale Seaford Wetlands, a pony club, entrance to Patterson Lakes
Navigation tips: From Mordialloc Station, walk along Bear St and turn left (southwards) to go along the Nepean Highway. At 0.5 km, cross Mordialloc Creek and follow the trail along the creek. At 1.3 km, take the right fork called the Long Beach Trail. At 6.4 km, after crossing Thames Promenade, take the right fork (westwards) and walk through the Chelsea Bicentennial Park (southwards). At 8.6 km you will reach Patterson River. Turn right (westwards to the sea) and follow the trail. At 10.5 km cross Patterson River and walk along Station St. At 11.6 km turn left (eastwards) into Eel Race Rd, At 11.9 km, cross Kananook Creek and turn right to get onto Kananook Creek Trail. At 12.6 km, cross the railway tracks and continue along the creek. At 17.3 km cross the Nepean Highway very carefully because of high-speed traffic. The trail continues on the other side of the creek. At 18.0 km, cross the footbridge and continue along the creek. At 18.6 km, you will reach Beach Rd. Turn left and head towards Frankston Station.

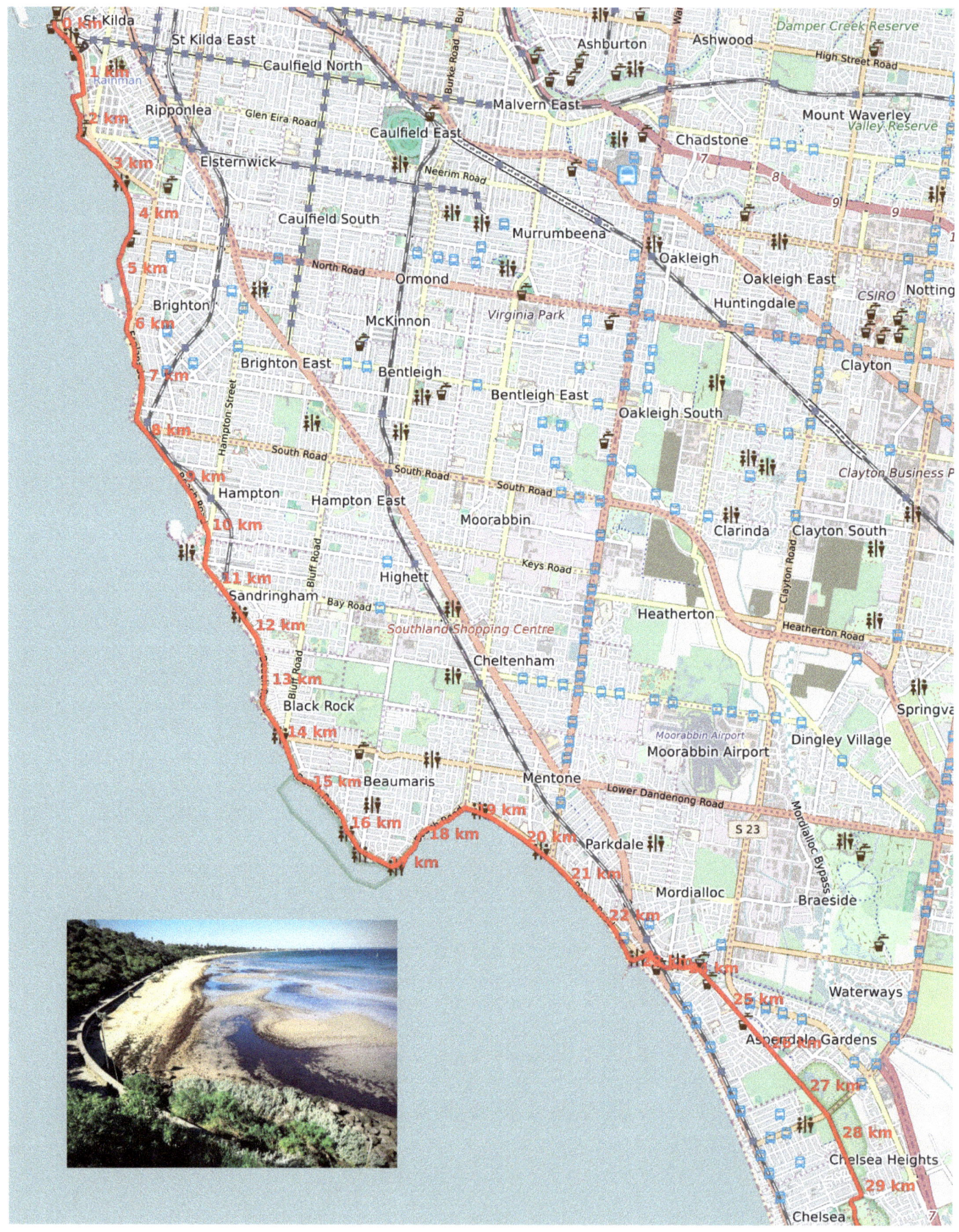

Map 28 - St Kilda to Frankston Marathon

This map is a combination of Maps 26 and 27. See those maps for detailed directions. I've done this map with my walking group during winter. It was scenic but terribly windy at the coastal parts!

Distance: 42.3 km one-way
Elevation: 1 to 28 metres above sea level. Peak elevation is at the 12.7 km mark, near Black Rock.
Start point: St Kilda Pier (near trams 3, 16, and 96)
End point: Frankston Station
Be alert: See Maps 26 and 27
Try to spot: See Maps 26 and 27

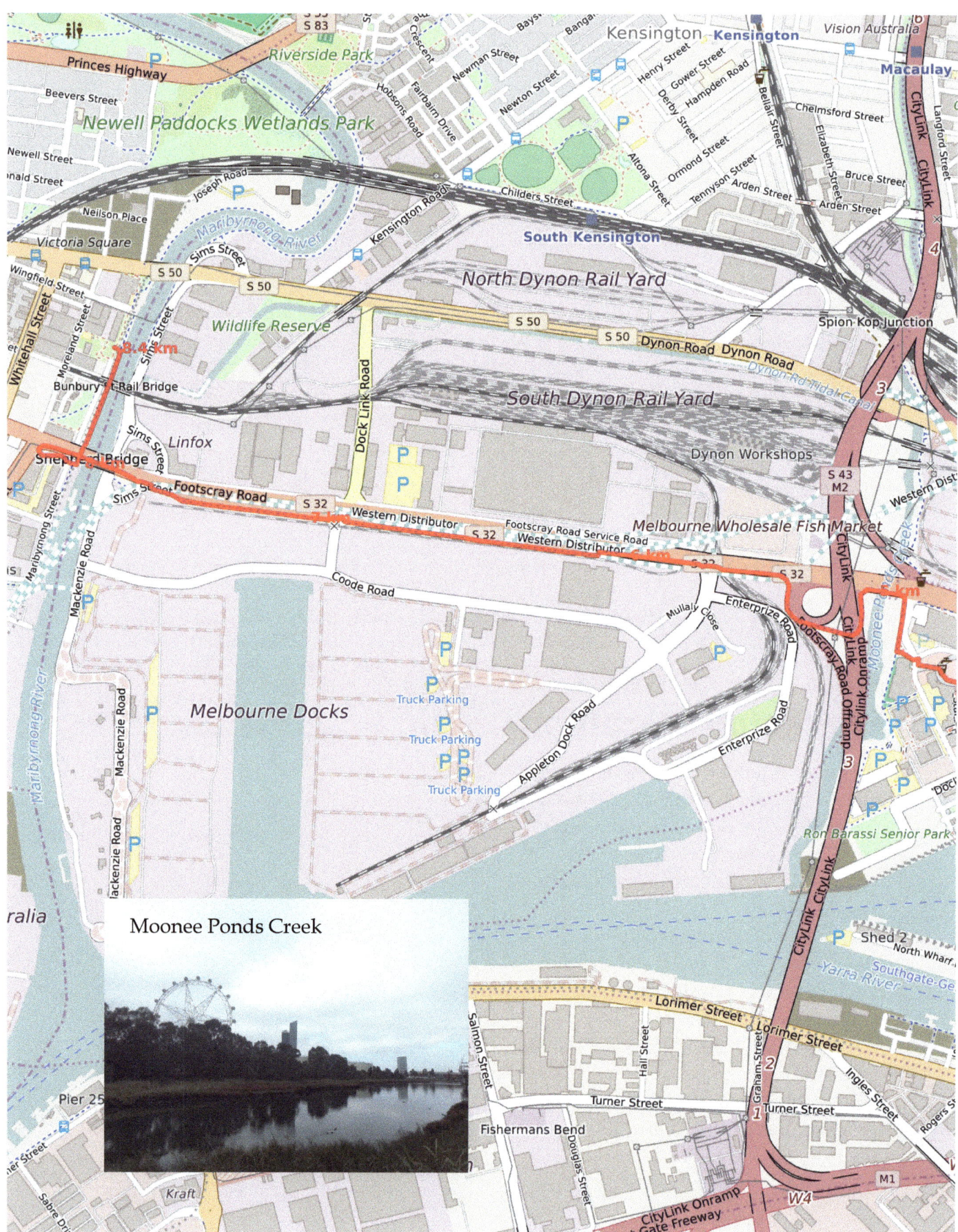

Map 29 - City to Footscray

I love the variety of scenery in this walk. You start with the busy cityscape, then go into the marinas of Docklands, then you walk along the busy industrial Port Of Melbourne and finish in the multicultural community of Footscray.

Distance: 8.3 km one-way (16.6 km return)

Elevation: 1 to 10 metres above sea level. Peak elevation is at Docklands.

Start point: Federation Square

End Point: Footscray Community Arts Centre, 600 metres from Footscray Station.

Be alert: Road crossings at Queensbridge St (traffic lights), Spencer St (traffic lights), Navigation Dr, Collins St (traffic lights), Bourke St (traffic lights), Docklands Dr, Pearl River Rd, Appleton Dock Rd (traffic lights), Docklands Hwy (traffic lights), Dock Link Rd (traffic lights), exit off Footscray Rd to Sims St, entry to Footscray Rd from Sims St (traffic lights)

Try to spot: Melbourne Star (ferris wheel), mouth of Moonee Ponds Creek, the Port Of Melbourne, the Maribyrnong River.

Navigation tips: From Federation Square, cross to the south bank of the Yarra River. At 2.4 km, cross over Webb Bridge to Docklands. At 4.5 km, you will be at the Melbourne Star ferris wheel. Cross Pearl River Rd and follow the cycling track that parallels Footscray Rd. After crossing the Maribyrnong River, walk north along it to the backyard of the Arts Centre.

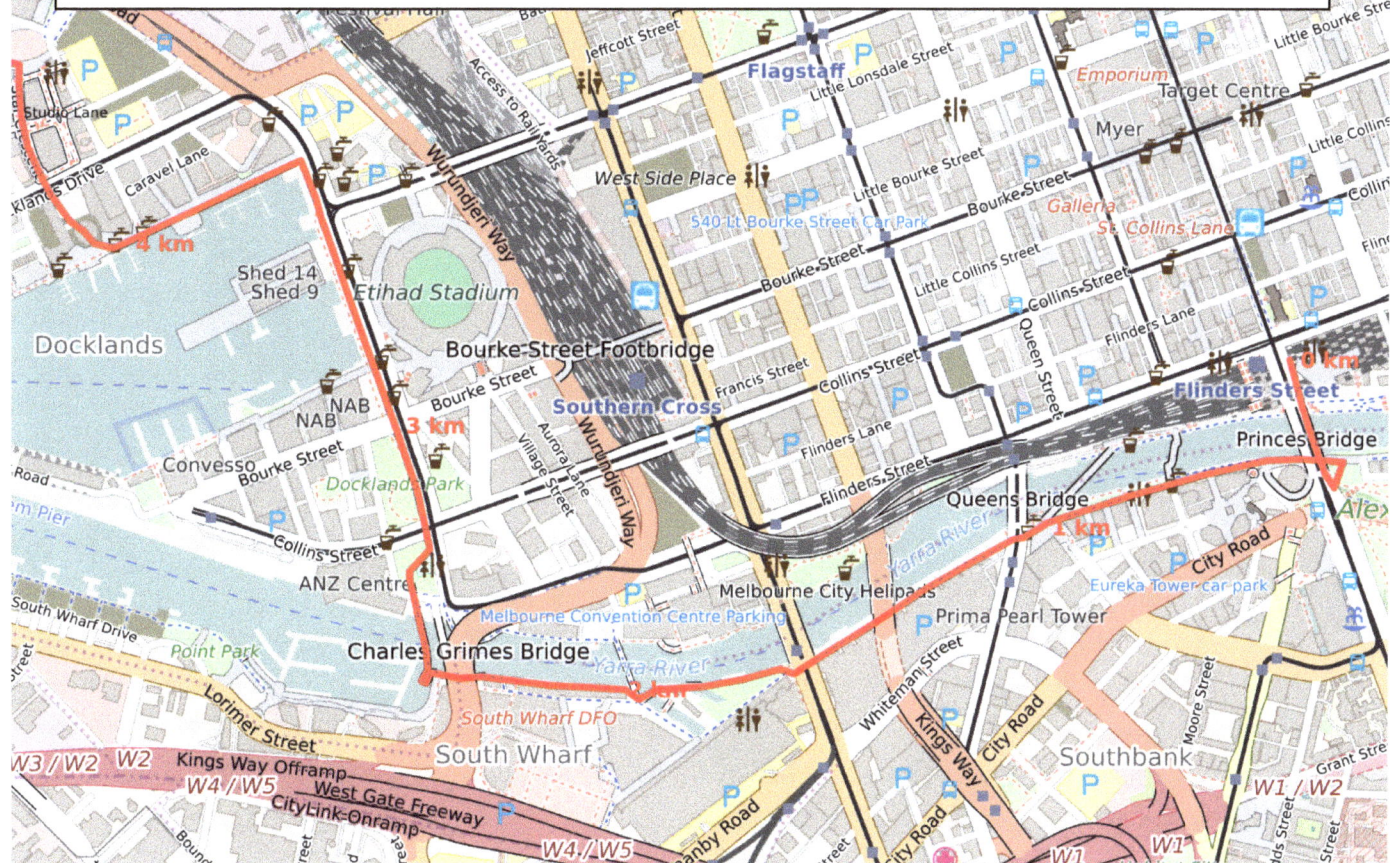

Map 30 - Footscray to Williamstown

Named after UK's King William IV, Williamstown is a beautiful coastal town and this is one of the best coastal walks in Melbourne. The first half of the walk is through industrial areas but the scenery would soon open up.

Distance: 8.2 km one-way (16.4 km return)

Elevation: 1 to 14 metres above sea level. Peak is at 2.3 km.

Start point: Footscray Community Arts Centre, 600 metres from Footscray Station.

End point: Commonwealth Reserve, Williamstown. 700 metres from Williamstown Station.

Be alert: Road crossings at Youell St, Whitehall St, Somerville Rd (traffic lights), Hall St, Leek St, Earsdon St, Frederick St, Little Hyde St, Taylor St, Francis St (traffic lights), carpark entrance near Greenwich Reserve, carpark entrance of The Anchorage Marina, carpark entrance of Williamstown Sailing Club, carpark entrance of Hobsons Bay Yacht Club, carpark entrance of Royal Victorian Motor Yacht Club

Try to spot: West Gate Bridge, West Gate Bridge Memorial, Scienceworks, HMAS Castlemaine

Navigation tips: Follow the Maribyrnong River Trail southwards. At 1.0 km, you will reach Whitehall St. Cross Whitehall St at a safe spot and then cut diagonally across Yarraville Gardens. Walk along Hyde St until you go under the West Gate Bridge. At this point the trail becomes the Hobsons Bay Coastal Trail. Follow it all the way to Williamstown. I like to stop and look at HMAS Castlemaine, which served during World War II and is now a museum.

West Gate Bridge

Map 31 - Maribyrnong River (one-way)

The Maribyrnong River starts in the Macedon Ranges (northwest of Melbourne) and it flows more than 60 km to meet the Yarra River. In this walk, you will see the final 7 km of the Maribyrnong River, where it flows through parks, golf courses, residential areas and the industrial port areas. If you have time, Poynton's Nursery is a great place to browse.

Distance: 12.2 km one-way

Elevation: 1 to 42 metres above sea level. Peak elevation is at the end.

Start point: Footscray Community Arts Centre, about 600 metres from Footscray Station.

End point: Moonee Ponds Station

Be alert: Road crossings at Anglers Way, Afton St carpark, The Boulevard, Bruce St, Cheffers St, Waverley St, Huntly St, Norfolk St, Sussex St, Hudson St, York St, Chester St, Grace St, Mantell St, Grosvenor St, Sydenham St, Norwood Crescent.

Try to spot: Flemington Racecourse, a red footbridge, a full-sized giraffe sculpture in someone's backyard, Afton St footbridge, Poynton's Nursery

Navigation tips: Head north along the Maribyrnong River Trail. At 7.3 km, cross Afton Street footbridge and cut through the carpark to Riverside Park. Go uphill to a lookout point. Then get back down and walk on the other side of the Maribyrnong River, heading east. Grab a coffee at Poynton's Nursery if you have time. Then continue along the river. Cross The Boulevard before you reach Essendon Rowing Club and head east along Holmes Rd. Continue along Holmes Rd for 1.5 km and you will reach Moonee Ponds Station.

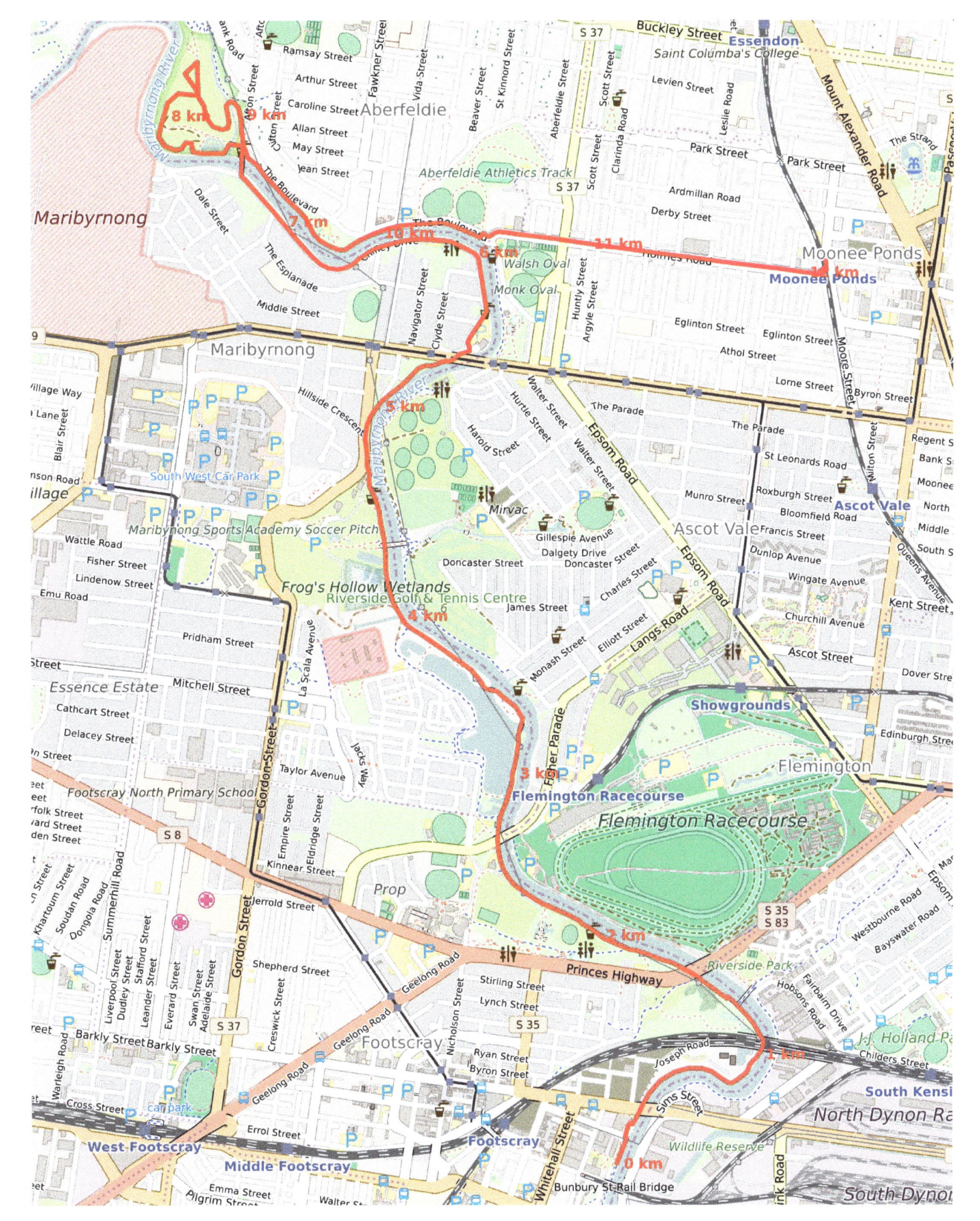

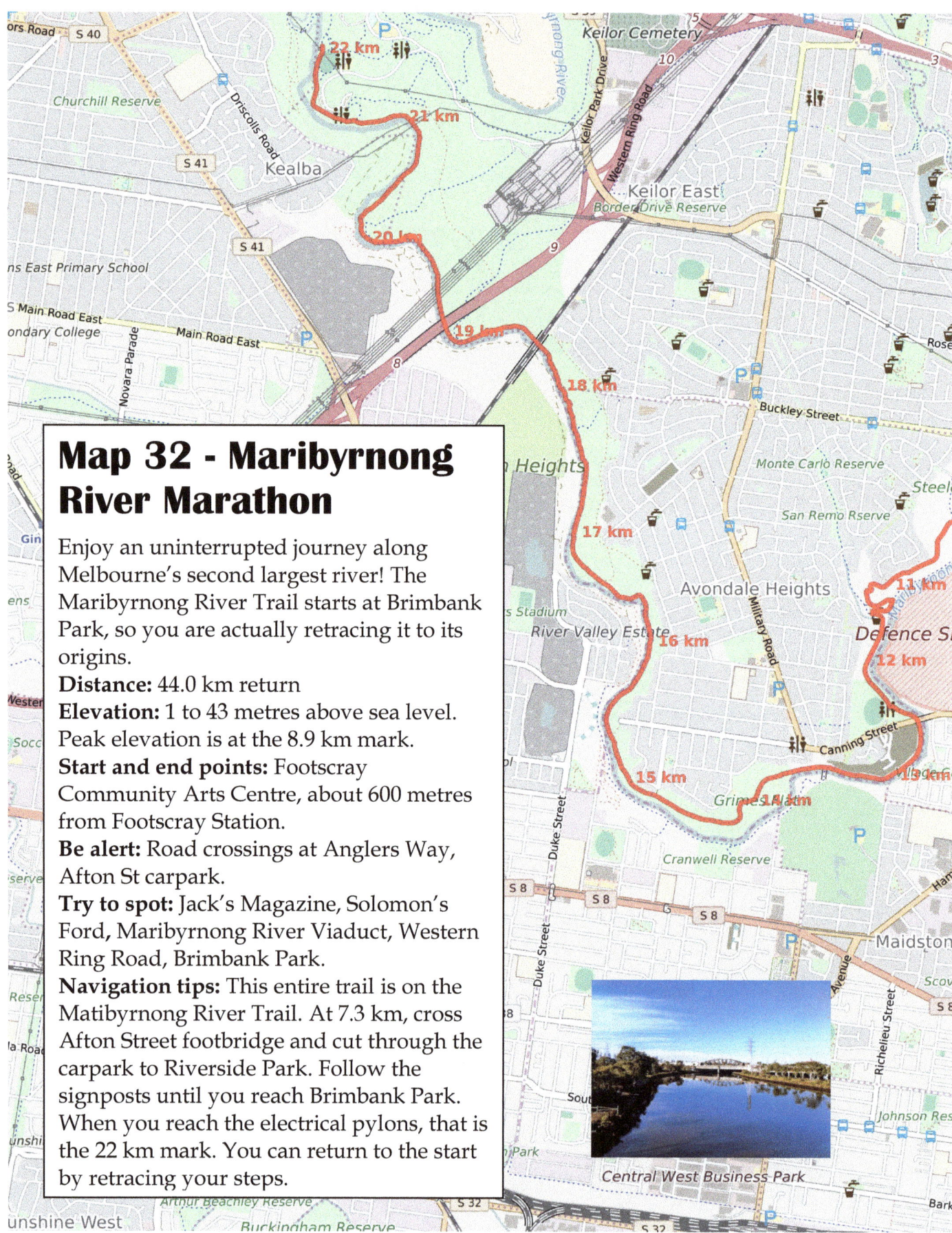

Map 32 - Maribyrnong River Marathon

Enjoy an uninterrupted journey along Melbourne's second largest river! The Maribyrnong River Trail starts at Brimbank Park, so you are actually retracing it to its origins.

Distance: 44.0 km return

Elevation: 1 to 43 metres above sea level. Peak elevation is at the 8.9 km mark.

Start and end points: Footscray Community Arts Centre, about 600 metres from Footscray Station.

Be alert: Road crossings at Anglers Way, Afton St carpark.

Try to spot: Jack's Magazine, Solomon's Ford, Maribyrnong River Viaduct, Western Ring Road, Brimbank Park.

Navigation tips: This entire trail is on the Matibyrnong River Trail. At 7.3 km, cross Afton Street footbridge and cut through the carpark to Riverside Park. Follow the signposts until you reach Brimbank Park. When you reach the electrical pylons, that is the 22 km mark. You can return to the start by retracing your steps.

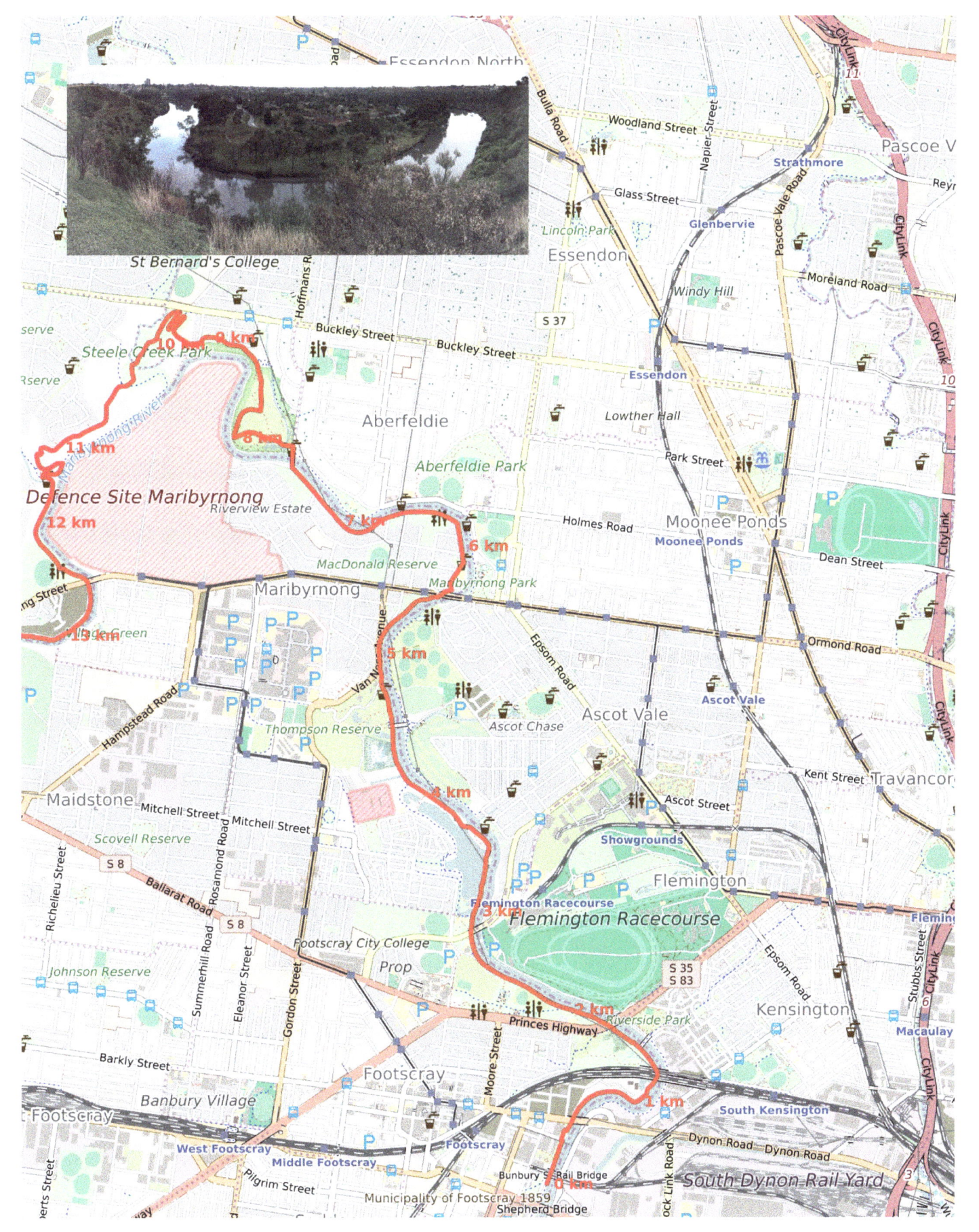

Map 33 - Williamstown to Altona

Altona is named after a German town near Hamburg. You will pass through important conservation areas and wetlands in this trail.

Distance: 10.7 km one-way (21.4 km return)

Elevation: 1 to 6 metres above sea level. Peak elevation is at the start.

Start point: Williamstown Station

End point: Altona Pier (about 400 metres from Altona Station).

Be alert: Road crossings at Battery Rd, carpark entrance at Beach Dressing Pavilion, carpark entrance of Williamstown Swimming & Lifesaving Club, Maddox Rd, carpark at Altona Boat Ramp

Try to spot: Williamstown Botanic Gardens, an oil refinery, Altona Coastal Park Conservation Reserve, Altona Pier

Navigation tips: From Williamstown Station, walk down Railway Terrace to get to the coast. You will be using the Hobsons Bay Coastal Trail for this walk, also known as Bay Trail West. At 2.5 km, you can go either way around the Williamstown Swimming & Lifesaving Club. At 7.0 km, the trail forks. Take the left fork as it is slightly shorter (the forks eventually meet). Stop at Altona Pier. And do enjoy a coffee in the town centre!

100 Steps Of Federation

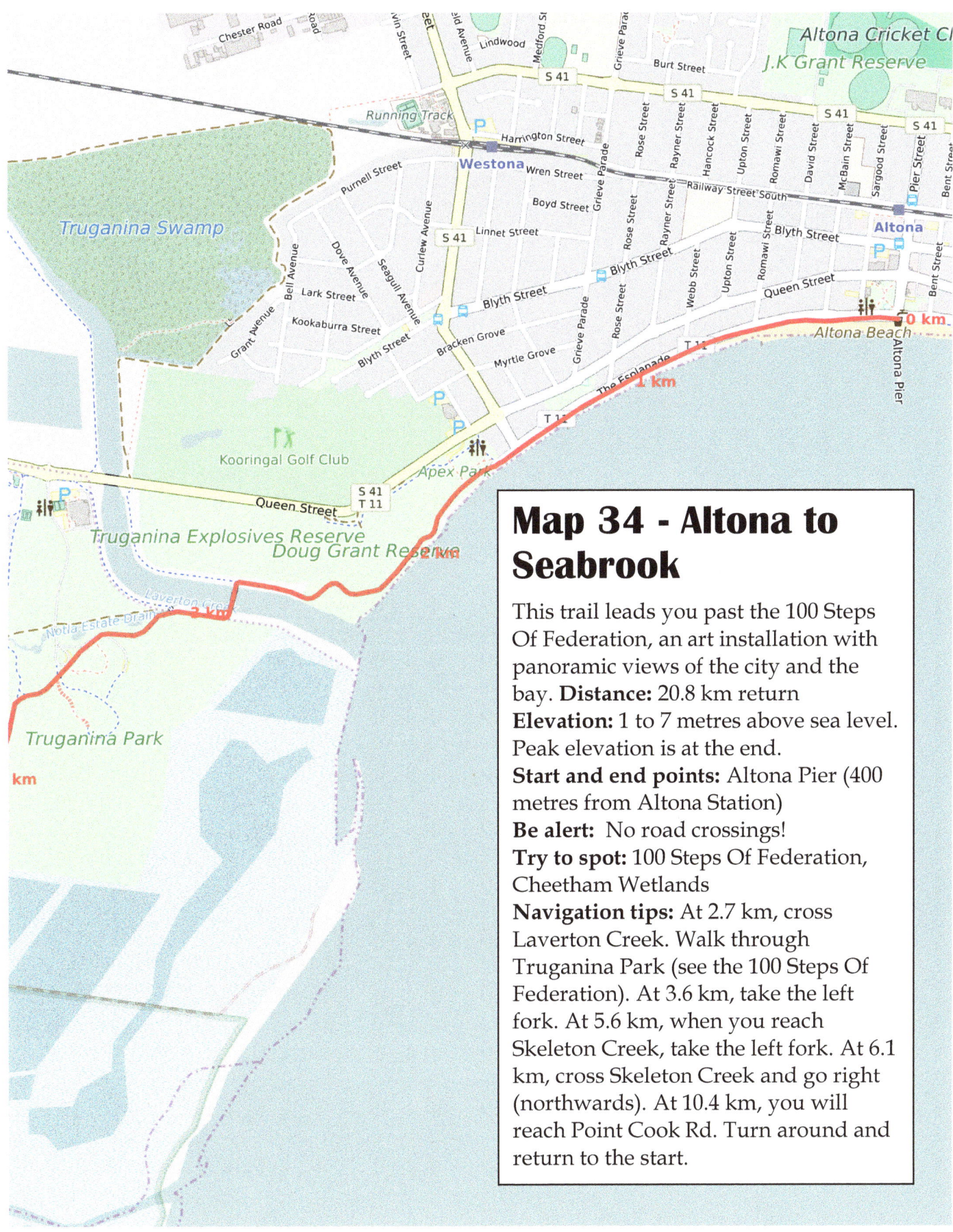

Map 34 - Altona to Seabrook

This trail leads you past the 100 Steps Of Federation, an art installation with panoramic views of the city and the bay. **Distance:** 20.8 km return
Elevation: 1 to 7 metres above sea level. Peak elevation is at the end.
Start and end points: Altona Pier (400 metres from Altona Station)
Be alert: No road crossings!
Try to spot: 100 Steps Of Federation, Cheetham Wetlands
Navigation tips: At 2.7 km, cross Laverton Creek. Walk through Truganina Park (see the 100 Steps Of Federation). At 3.6 km, take the left fork. At 5.6 km, when you reach Skeleton Creek, take the left fork. At 6.1 km, cross Skeleton Creek and go right (northwards). At 10.4 km, you will reach Point Cook Rd. Turn around and return to the start.

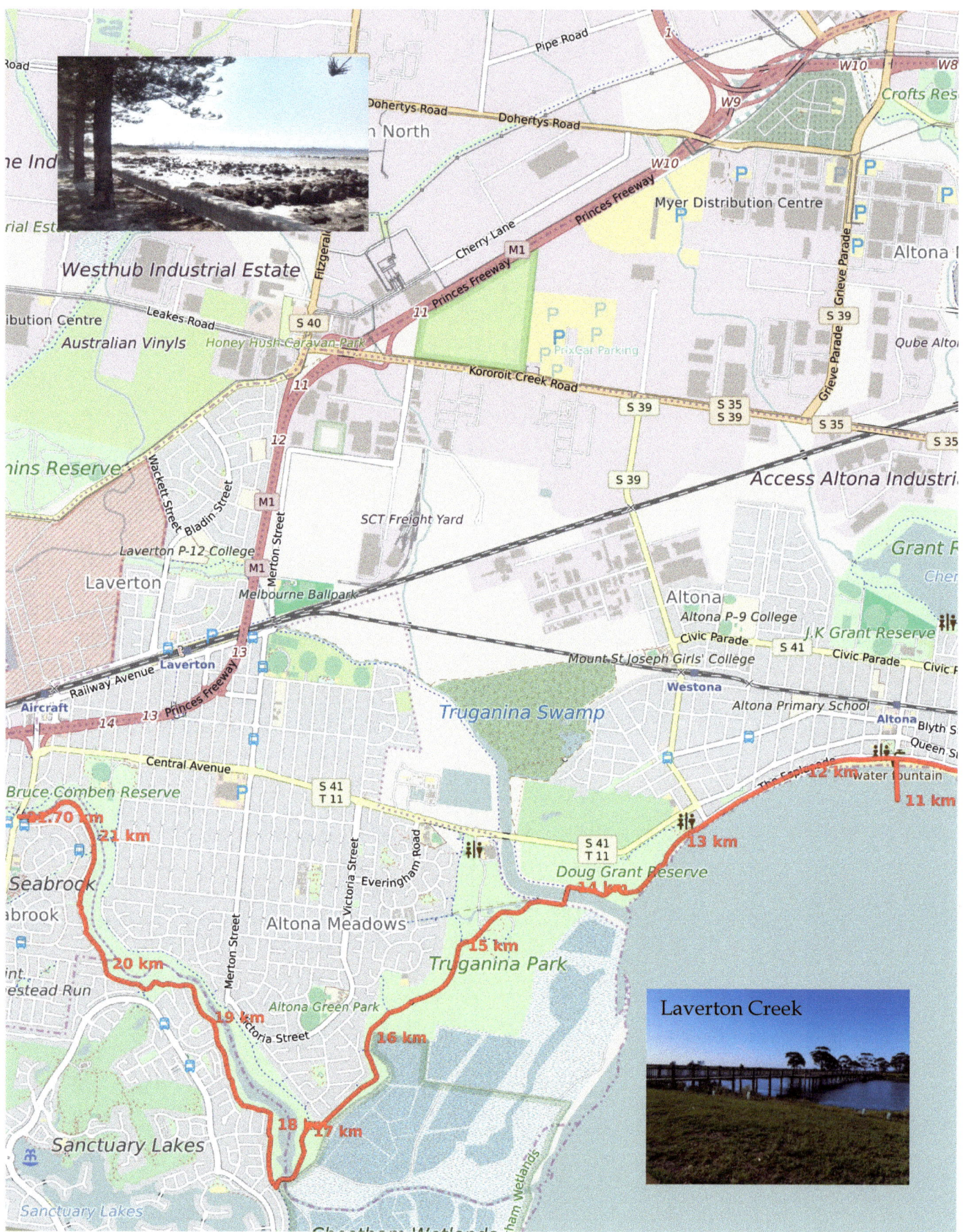

Map 35 - Williamstown Marathon

This map is a combination of Maps 33 and 34. See those maps for detailed directions. This is a great trail to do if you want to do a marathon distance. There are many toilets and drinking fountains, and the coastal scenery is amazing.

Distance: 43.4 km return.

Elevation: 1 to 7 metres above sea level. Peak elevation is at the end.

Start and end points: Williamstown Station

Be alert: See Maps 33 and 34

Try to spot: See Maps 33 and 34

Navigation tips: Similar to Maps 33 and 34, but for this trail I'm adding walking up and down Altona Pier to get the extra distance and to enjoy the view.

Map 36 - Werribee Mansion & Winery

This trail features a river, a mansion, a rose garden, and you can do wine tasting in the middle of it! To see the Victoria State Rose Garden at its best, visit in early November.

Distance: 14.5 km return

Elevation: 2 to 26 metres above sea level

Start and end points: Werribee Station   **Be alert:** No road crossings!

Try to spot: Werribee Bowling Club, the perimeter of Werribee Zoo, Werribee Mansion, Victoria State Rose Garden, Shadowfax Winery

Navigation tips: At 3.1 km, when you reach Princes Freeway, cross the bridge over the river and then go under the freeway from the west side of the river. At 5.7 km, do not go straight but turn left to descend towards the river. At 6.1 km, at the fork, go left and cross the river. At 6.6 km, at the fork, go right and you will soon enter the grounds of the mansion. At the mansion, don't forget to visit the Victoria State Rose Garden. After that, walk 300 metres south along South Drive to Shadowfax Winery. Follow the same path to return to Werribee Station.

Werribee Mansion

Werribee River

Victoria State Rose Garden

Map 37 – Woodend Winery

This is a peaceful walk amidst trees and hills, with wine-tasting in the middle! It's one of my favourite out-of-Melbourne walks. If you have time after the walk, consider visiting Mount Macedon or Hanging Rock.

Distance: 9.4 km return

Elevation: 567 to 630 metres above sea level. Peak elevation is at the winery.

Start and end points: Woodend Station

Be alert: Road crossings at Calder Highway, Plants Lane, Bawden Rd

Try to spot: Woodend township, the Calder Freeway, Mount Macedon Winery

Navigation tips: Woodend Station is only an hour by V-Line train from Southern Cross Station. From Woodend Station, cross High Street and walk along the railway line (on the north side). At 3.2 km, go under the Calder Freeway and walk along Bawden Rd. You will be walking along Bawden Rd itself (no pavement) so watch out for cars. At 4.1 km, take the left fork and at 4.4 km, you will see the gate of the winery. Walk up the driveway about 300 metres and you will find the cellar doors. Have some wine-tasting or coffees while enjoying views of the vines. Then retrace your steps to get back to Woodend Station.

Map 38 - Boathouse to Boathouse

The bustle of the city will feel very far away during this scenic river walk. Studley Park Boathouse is the oldest public boathouse on the Yarra River, while Fairfield Park Boathouse was built on the grounds of the Yarra Bend Hospital of the Insane.

Distance: 9.0 km circuit.

Elevation: 5 to 49 metres above sea level. Peak elevation is at a lookout point at Yarra Boulevard, at 8.2 km.

Start and end points: Fairfield Boathouse (500 metres from Dennis Railway Station)

Be alert: Road crossing at Yarra Bend Rd, Boathouse Rd, road to Bell Bird Park, and a few driveways on Yarra Boulevard.

Try to spot: Fairifield Pipe Bridge, Dights Falls, Kanes Bridge and bats sleeping in the trees.

Navigation tips: From the carpark at Fairfield Boathouse, take the Main Yarra Trail towards the city. After crossing Yarra Bend Rd, take the left fork towards the city. At 1.7 km, do not cross the footbridge, instead go left and head towards Studley Boathouse. Stay close to the Yarra River from this point. At 2.8 km, make a sharp hairpin turn to keep close to the river. At 3.7 km, cross Kanes Bridge. Studley Boathouse is 200 metres to your right after crossing. When you are ready to leave Studley Boathouse, walk back towards Kanes Bridge and cross the carpark entrance and follow the footpath uphill. At 4.5 km, you will reach Yarra Boulevard. Cross Boathouse Rd and walk along Yarra Boulevard (heading eastwards). At 6.4 km, keep going along Yarra Boulevard, don't follow the road that leads Bell Bird Park. At 7.8 km, you will cross over the Eastern Freeway. At 8.2 km, you will reach a lookout point (Wurundjeri Spur Lookout) with views of the city. Leave Yarra Boulevard and head downwards back towards Fairfield Boathouse. Cross the pipe bridge and go up towards the starting point.

Fairfield Park Boathouse

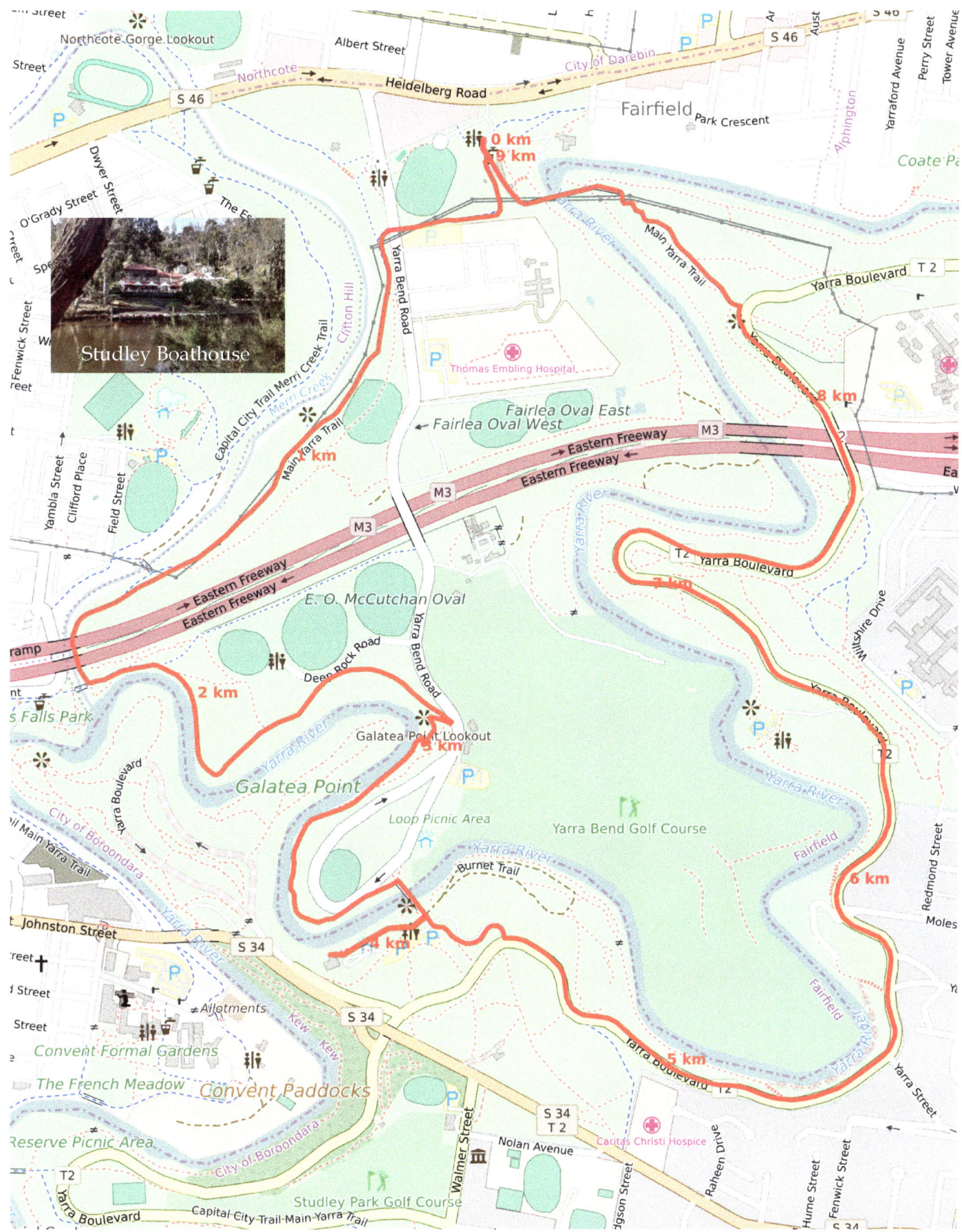

Map 39 - Farm to Two Boathouses

This is similar to Map 38, but with the additional of an urban farm! Its full name is Collingwood Children's Farm and it was established in 1979 to provide country experiences for city children.
Distance: 10.5 km circuit.
Elevation: 2 to 49 metres above sea level. Peak elevation is at 6.6 km.
Start and end points: Collingwood Farm. 900 metres from Victoria Park Station.
Surface: mix of gravel and pavement.
Be alert: Road crossings at road leading to Studley Park Rd, road leading to Yarra Boulevard, Boathouse Rd, road to Bell Bird Park, and a few driveways on Yarra Boulevard , Yarra Bend Rd.
Try to spot: Abbotsford Convent, Dights Falls, bats sleeping in the trees. You will be walking on Fairifield Pipe Bridge and Kanes Bridge on this route.
Navigation tips: Find the Main Yarra Trail which is just outside the farm entrance. Head towards the city. At 0.9 km, climb the steps and cross the river. Go straight to Yarra Boulevard, do not follow the Main Yarra Trail. At 1.1 km, you will reach Yarra Boulevard and turn left to head eastwards. At 2.0 km, cross two roads carefully. After crossing the second road, turn left. At 2.3 km, take the path that leads downwards to Studley Boathouse. From Studley Boathouse head towards Boathouse Rd and walk along the path beside it. At 2.9 km, you will reach Yarra Boulevard. Cross Boathouse Rd and walk along Yarra Boulevard (heading eastwards). At 4.8 km, keep going along Yarra Boulevard, don't follow the road that leads Bell Bird Park. At 6.2 km, you will cross over the Eastern Freeway. At 6.6 km, you will reach a lookout point with views of the city. Leave Yarra Boulevard and head downwards towards the river. Cross the pipe bridge and turn right towards Fairfield Boathouse. From Fairfield Boathouse, walk towards the carpark area and find the Main Yarra Trail heading back to the city. At 8.0 km, cross Yarra Bend Rd and take the left fork towards the city. At 9.4 km, cross the footbridge over Merri Creek and follow the river back to the start point. Don't forget to enjoy coffees at the farm's café or Abbotsford Convent next door.

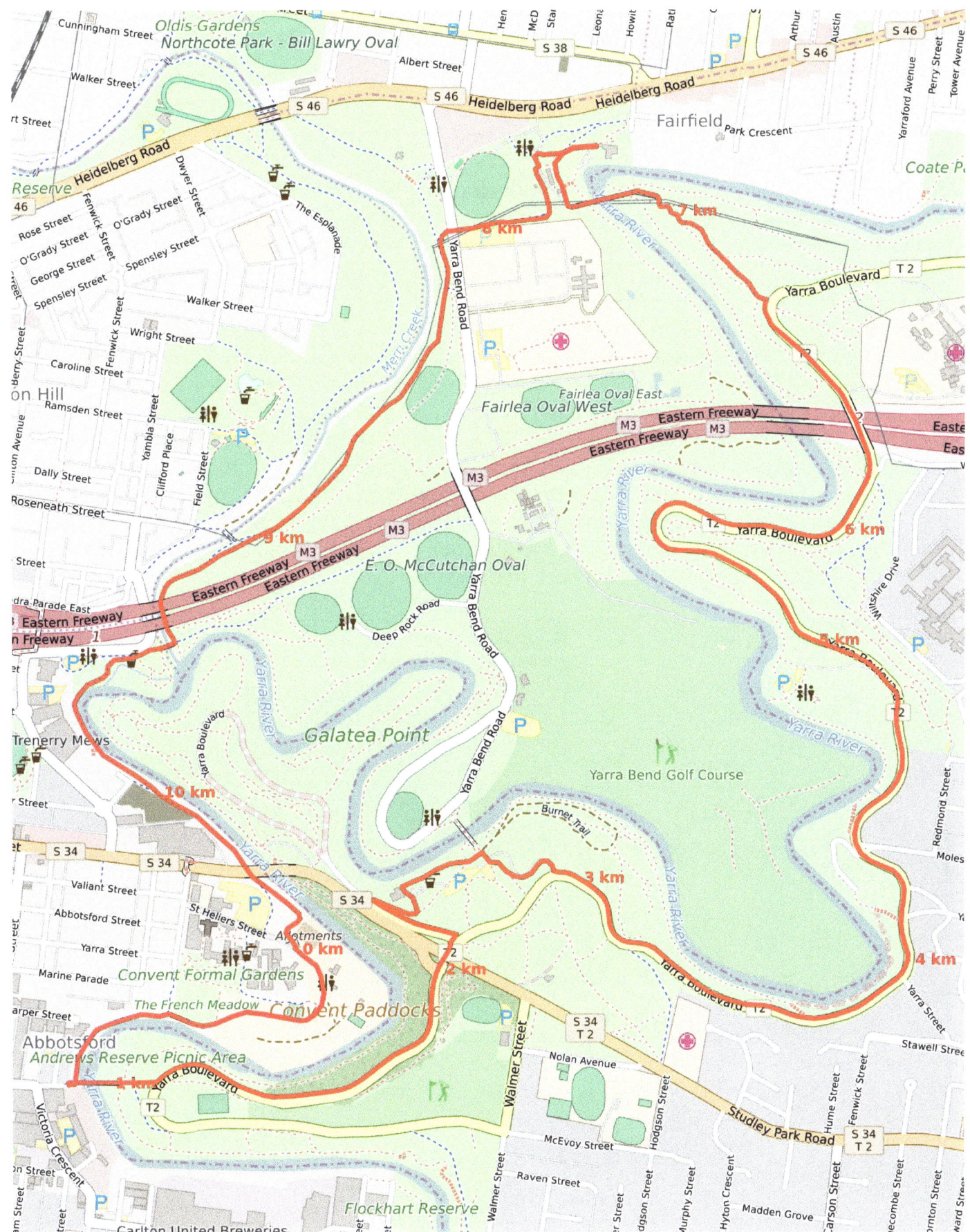

Map 40 – Collingwood Farm to Dights Falls

This trail is set in Yarra Bend Park, the largest natural bushland park in Melbourne. Dights Falls (pictured below) is an artificial weir on the Yarra River built in the 1840s. This area is a significant meeting place for the indigenous communities that lived here.

Distance: 7.8 km circuit.
Elevation: 2 to 46 metres above sea level. Peak elevation is at 1.9 km.
Start and end points: Collingwood Farm (900 metres from Victoria Park Station)
Be alert: Road crossings at road leading to Studley Park Rd, road leading to Yarra Boulevard,
Try to spot: Abbotsford Convent, Dights Falls and its fish ladder. You will be walking on Kanes Bridge on this route.
Navigation tips: Find the Main Yarra Trail which is just outside the farm entrance. Head towards the city. At 0.9 km, climb the steps and cross the river. Go straight to Yarra Boulevard, do not follow the Main Yarra Trail. At 1.1 km, you will reach Yarra Boulevard and turn left to head eastwards. At 2.0 km, cross two roads carefully. After crossing the second road, turn left. At 2.3 km, there is a path that leads downwards to Studley Boathouse, but don't take it yet. Instead go straight ahead and find the lookout point overseeing Dights Falls. Then return and go to Studley Boathouse. From Studley Boathouse, cross Kanes Bridge and turn left. Follow the river. At 5.4 km, make a sharp left turn and continue following the river. At 6.5km, cross the footbridge over Merri Creek and go left to take a good look at Dights Falls. Then go back to the Main Yarra Trail which will bring you back to the start.

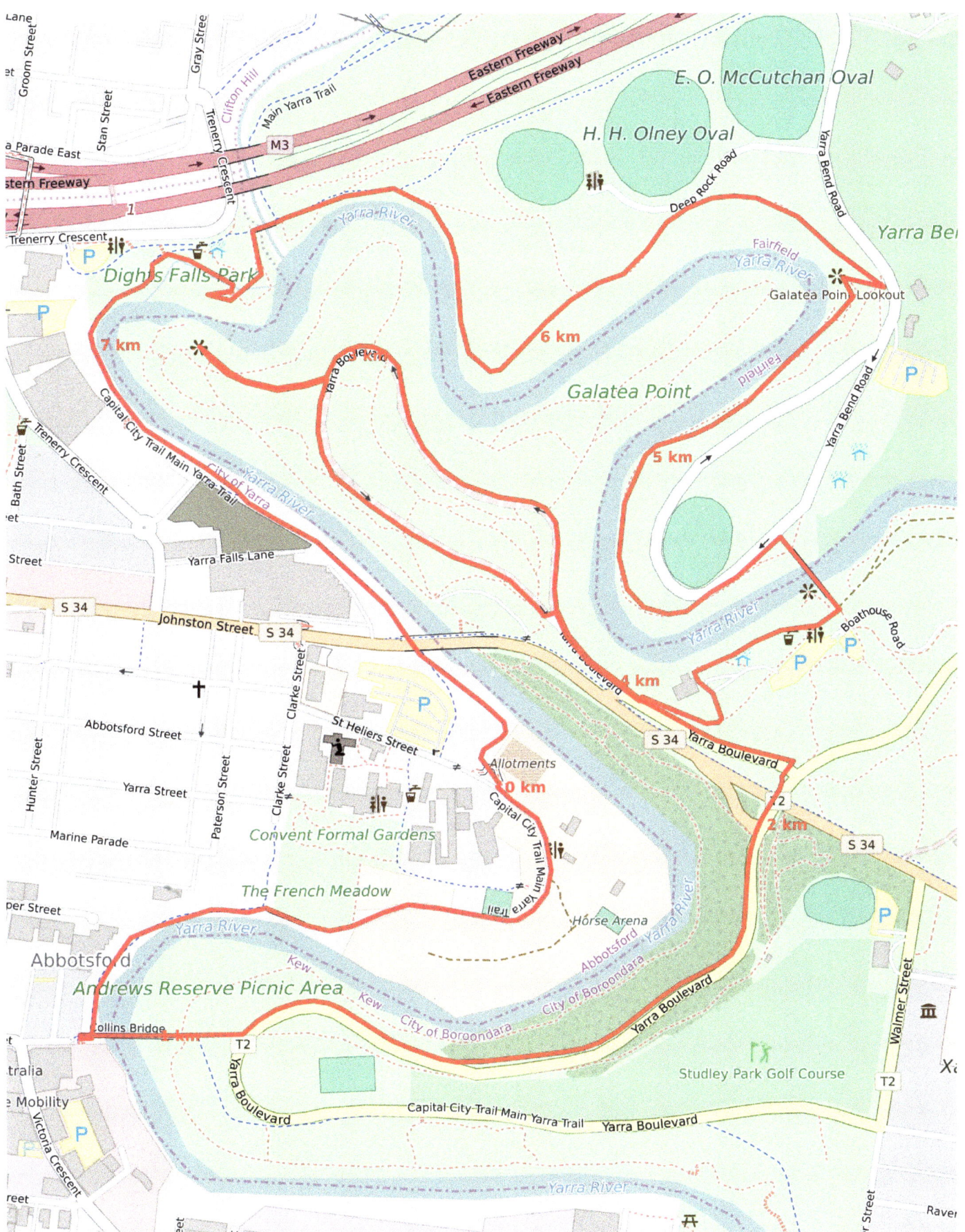

Map 41 - Collingwood Farm to CERES Community Environment Park

This trail goes along the Yarra River and Merri Creek to CERES. CERES used to be a bluestone quarry and later a municipal tip. Now it's a community organisation that aims to protect and enhance the natural environment by providing information and education to Melburnians. I often call this the 'farm-to-farm' walk.

Distance: 13.6 km return.

Elevation: 3 to 39 metres above sea level. Peak elevation is at 4.6 km.

Start and end points: Collingwood Farm. 900 metres from Victoria Park Station.

Be alert: This track has no road crossings!

Try to spot: Dights Falls, Rushall Community Garden, CERES (Centre for Education and Research in Environmental Studies)

Navigation tips: Just outside the entrance of Collingwood Farm is the Main Yarra Trail. Walk north along the trail. At 1.1 km, cross Merri Creek and go left to go under the Eastern Freeway. You are now on the Merri Creek Trail. At 1.5 km, cross Merri Creek again and go right. At 2.8 km, go downhill to go under Heidelberg Rd. At 4.2 km, you will reach Rushall Station. Go through the tunnel and turn right. At 4.6 km, turn right. At 5.2 km, you will reach St Georges Rd. Cross the creek and walk on the opposite side. At 6.8 km, CERES' back gate will be on your left.

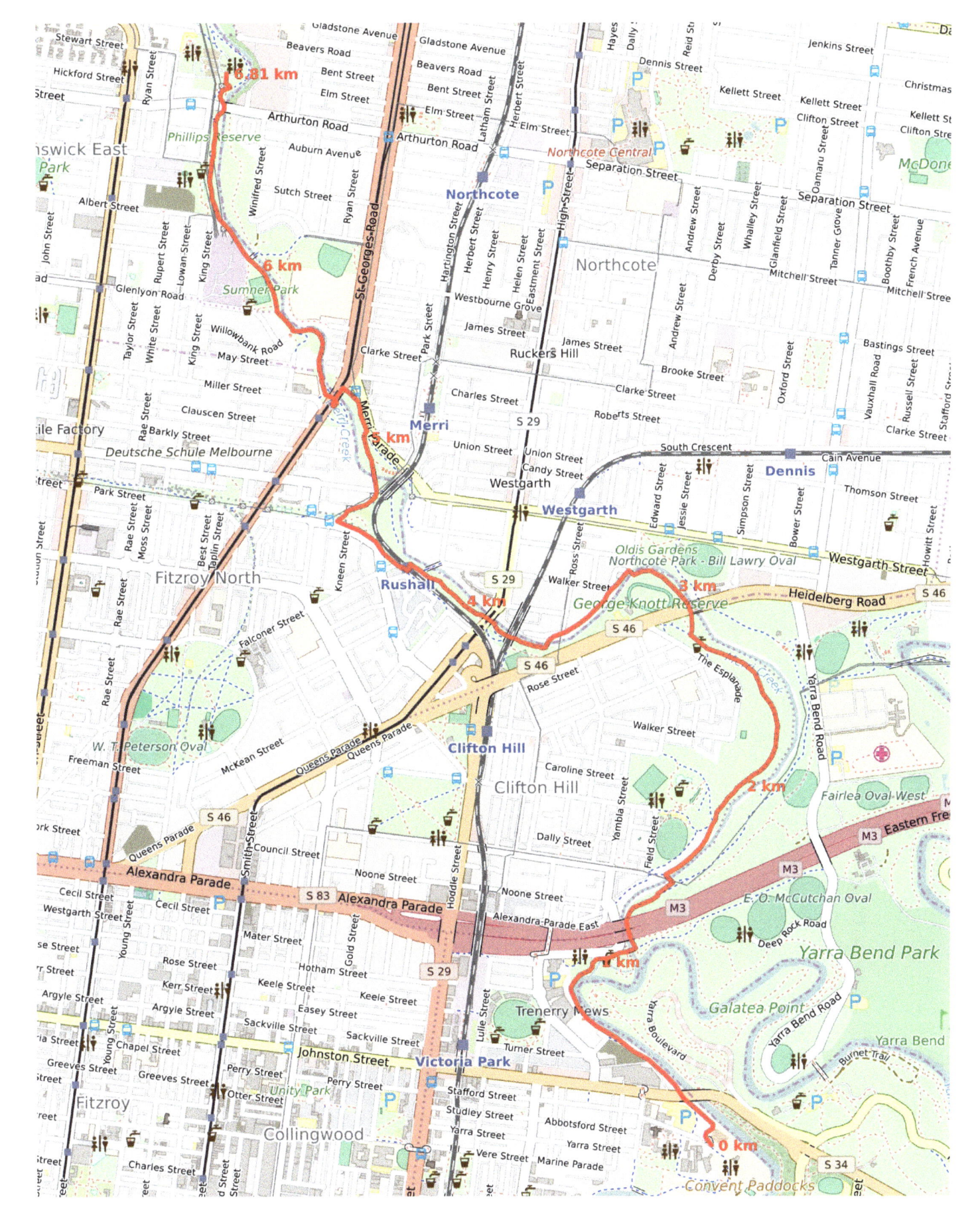

Map 42 - Triple Farm Walk

Here is a walk that encompasses three urban farms! Besides Collingwood Farm and CERES, we have Joe's Market Garden (now also run by CERES). Joe's is the last inner-city market garden in Melbourne. It was started by Chinese immigrants and has been in operation for over 150 years.

Distance: 10.0 km one-way (20.0 km return)

Elevation: 3 to 40 metres above sea level. Peak elevation is at 8.2 km, at Moreland Rd.

Start point: Collingwood Farm, 900 metres from Victoria Park Station

End point: CERES Joe's Market Garden, 200 metres away from Nicholson Street.

Be alert: No road crossings!

Try to spot: Brunswick Velodrome, a Russian orthodox church, Dights Falls

Navigation tips: The first 6.7 km is the same as Map 41. From inside CERES, exit at CERES north gate. At 8.1 km, after crossing under Moreland Rd, cross to the other side of Merri Creek. At 9.7 km, cross the footbridge and go right. Joe's Market Garden will be visible from here. To go back to the start by tram, go 200m west of the farm to Nicholson St and take the Number 1.

Joe's Market Garden

Russian Orthodox Church

CERES

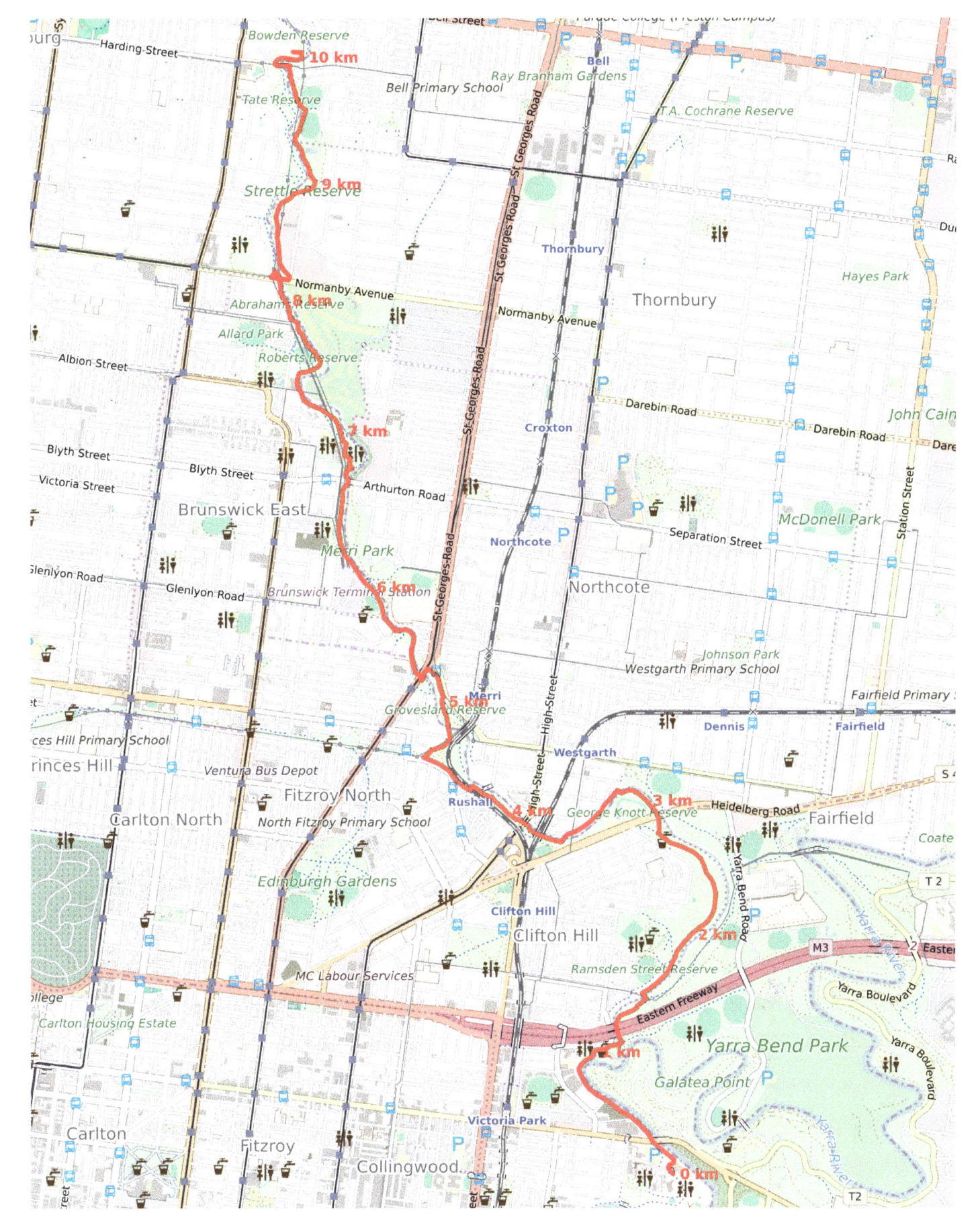

Map 43 - Fairfield Boathouse to Heide Museum

This lush and green trail follows the Yarra River upstream, with a narrow section that goes beside the Eastern Freeway. The end of the trail features the Heide Museum of Modern Art, established in 1981 by arts benefactors John and Sunday Reed in partnership with the Victorian Government.

Distance: 19.8 km return. If you want to leave the trail at the Heide, you can take a bus or walk westwards for 2 km to Heidelberg Station (visible on the map)

Elevation: 6 to 50 metres above sea level. Peak elevation is at the 0.8 km mark.

Start and end points: Fairfield Boathouse, about 500 metres from Dennis Railway Station.

Be alert: Road crossings at Belford Rd, Yarra Flats Entry Rd, road leading to Banksia Park.

Try to spot: Pipe bridge over the Yarra, Royal Talbot Rehabilitation Centre, sculpture park at the Heide grounds

Navigation tips: From the Fairfield Boathouse carpark, walk down towards the Yarra River. Cross the pipe bridge and go uphill. At 0.8 km, you will reach Yarra Boulevard. Go left (eastwards) and walk along Yarra Boulevard. At 1.4 km, leave Yarra Boulevard, go down the stairs and walk under the Chandler Highway. You will be walking along the Eastern Freeway for a few kilometres. At 5.6 km, before you reach Burke Rd, cross the footbridge and continue eastwards along the Main Yarra Trail. At 7.6 km, take the right fork. At 8.6 km, take the left fork and cross the river via Manningham Road West. After you cross the river, go under Manningham Road West and you will encounter another fork. Take the right fork. At 9.4 km, take the left fork. At 9.8 km, the public park of Heide Museum will be to your right.

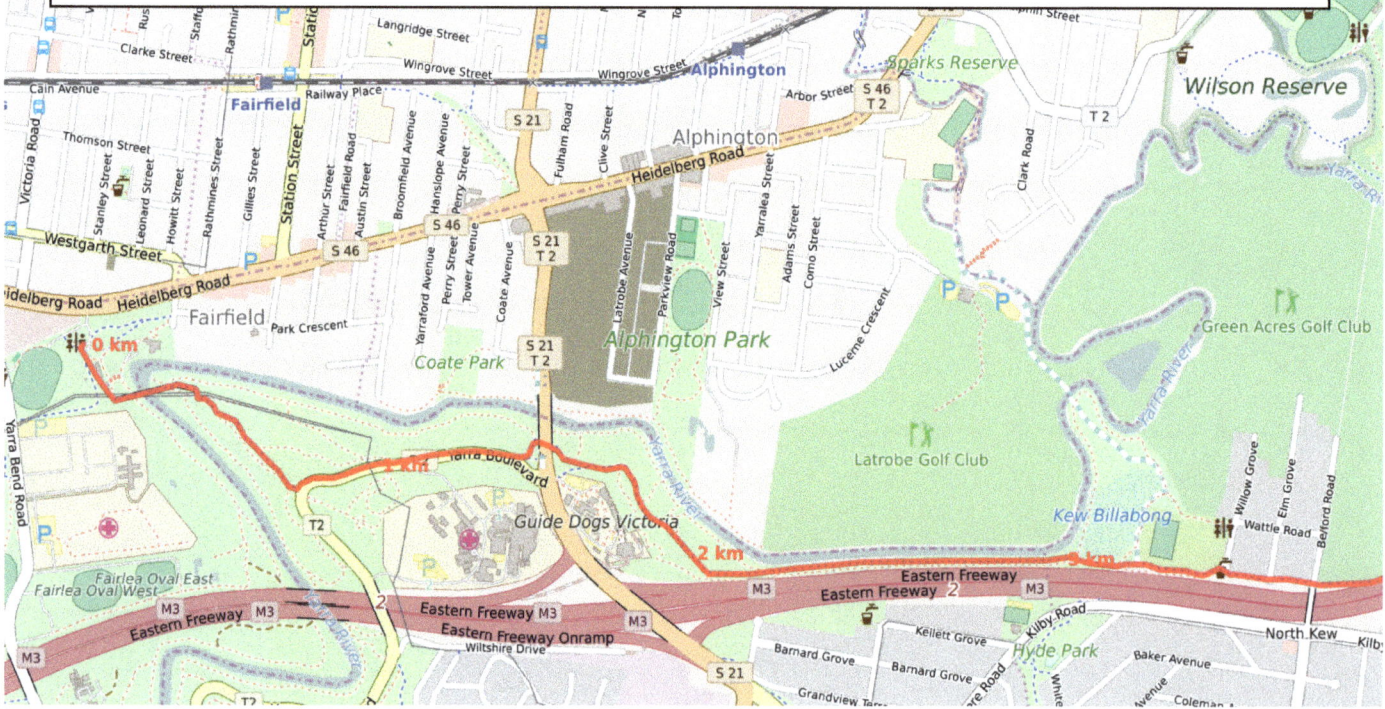

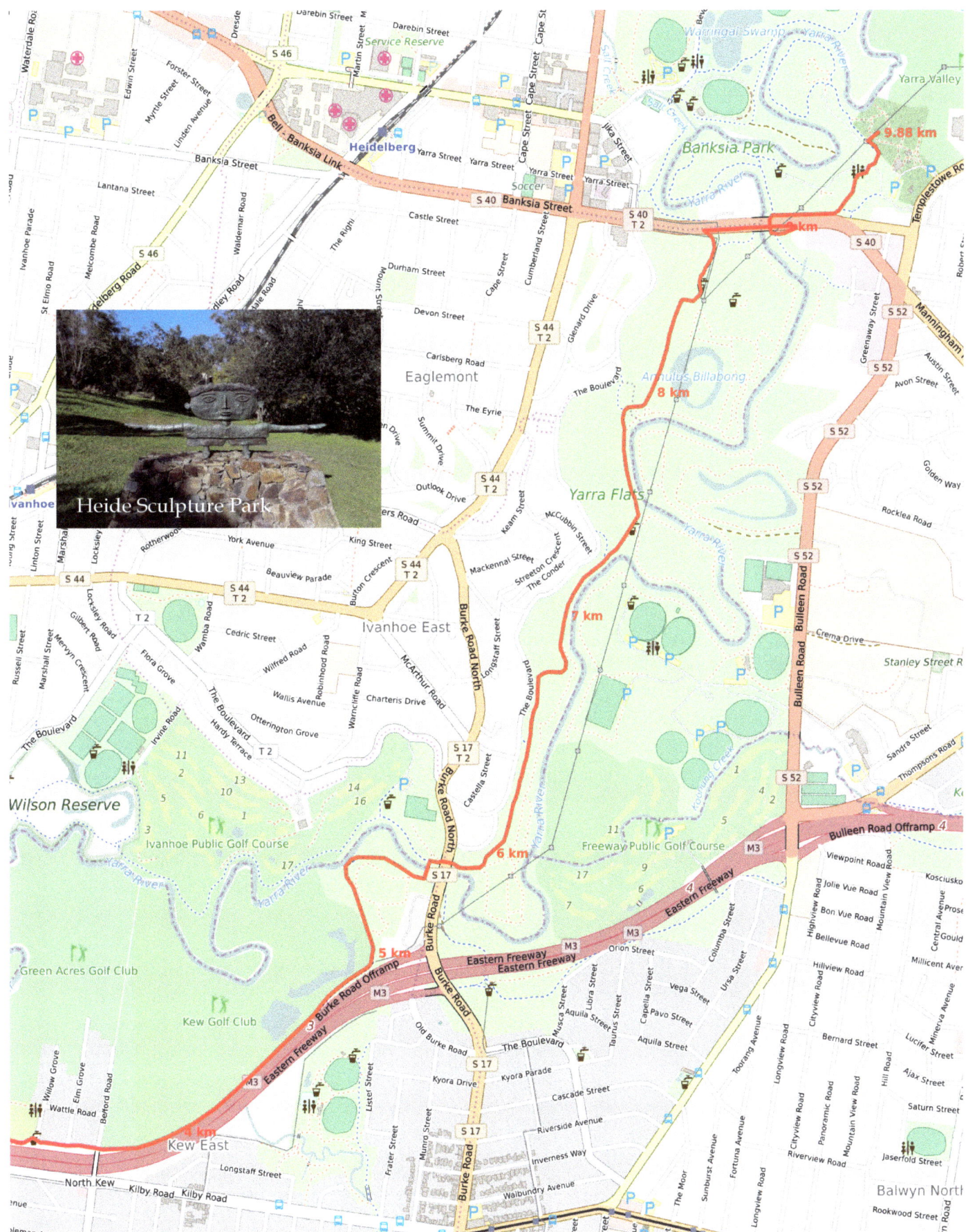
Heide Sculpture Park

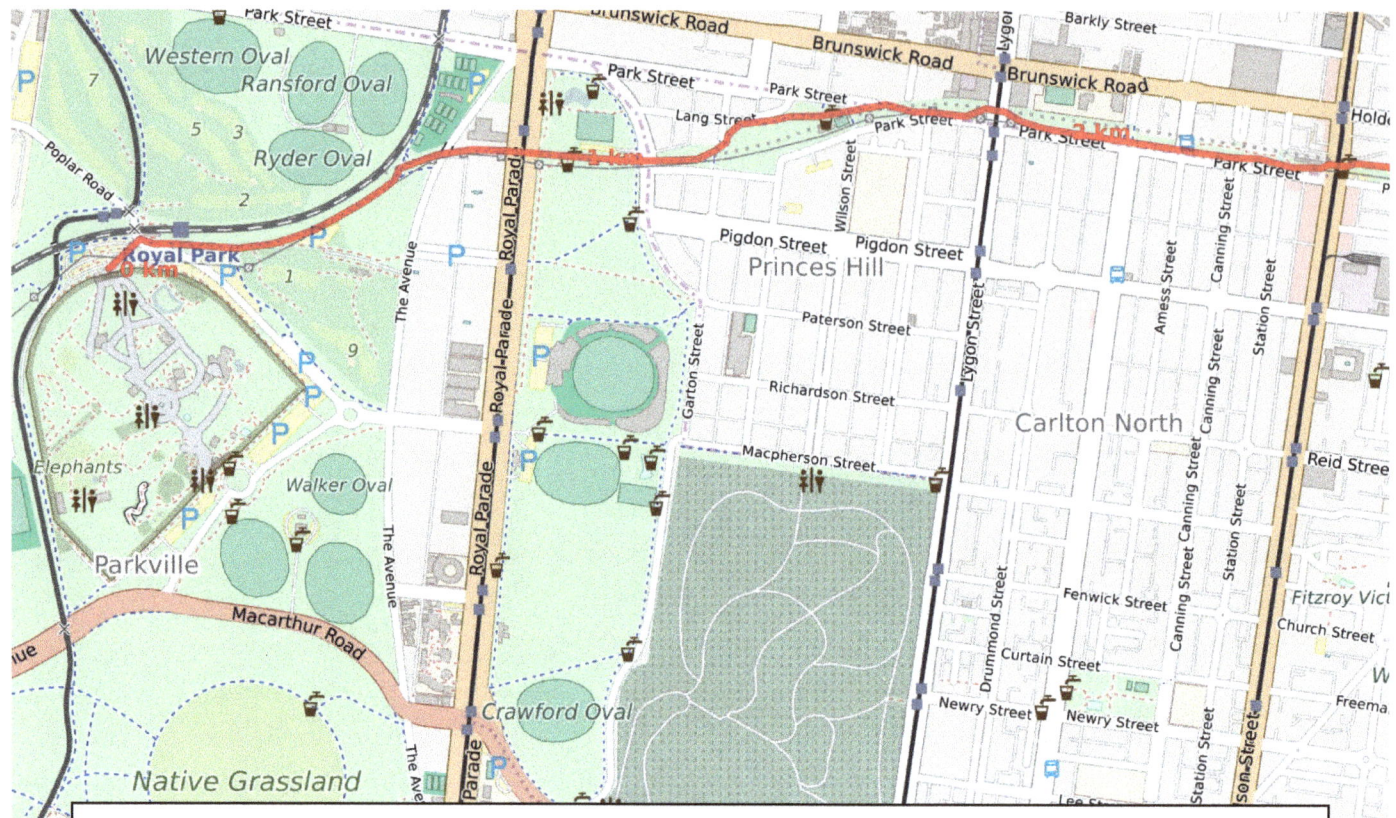

Map 44 - Zoo to Collingwood Farm

This trail starts and ends with two beloved institutions - the Melbourne Zoo and Collingwood Farm. Melbourne Zoo is Australia's oldest zoo. It has over 320 species and 5000 individual animals.

Distance: 8.2 km one-way (16.4 km return)

Elevation: 3 to 50 metres above sea level. Peak elevation is at the 0.4 km mark.

Start point: Melbourne Zoo back gate (north side), 50 metres from Royal Park Station.

End point: Collingwood Farm, 900 metres from Victoria Park Station.

Be alert: Road crossings at Poplar Rd, Bowen Crescent, Lygon St (traffic lights), Amess St, Nicholson St (traffic lights), Rae St, Brunswick St, St Georges Rd, Bennett St.

Try to spot: The old train tracks from the disused Inner Circle Line.

Navigation tips: From the Melbourne Zoo back gate, get onto the Capital City Trail just outside Royal Park Station. At 0.6 km, there is a triple fork, take the middle one that goes to a tunnel under Royal Parade. At 3.5 km, there is a fork but continue straight. At 3.8 km, cross the train tracks at Rushall Station by going through the tunnel. At 5.3 km, cross under Heidelberg Rd and go up a steep slope and go left (south-east). At 6.3 km, take the left fork and at 6.6 km, cross the footbridge and turn right (westwards), At 7.0 km, turn right and cross the footbridge over Merri Creek. Go another 1 km and you will reach Collingwood Farm.

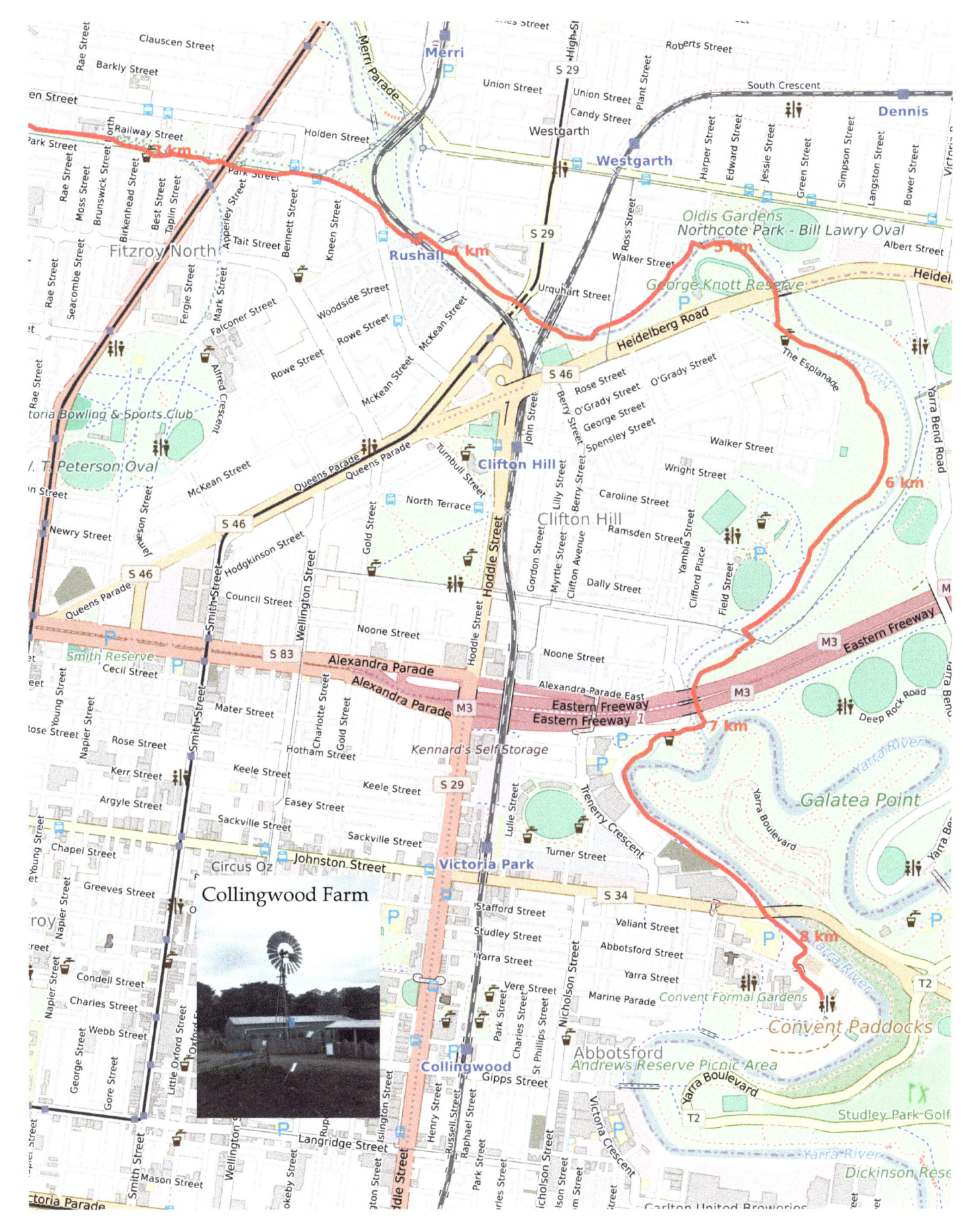

Map 45 - Zoo to CERES

This route follows the Inner Circle Line Trail and then turns north onto the Merri Creek Trail. At CERES, take the time to enjoy the rows of crops, the café, the organic grocery store and the nursery.

Distance: 11.8 km return.

Elevation: 27 to 50 metres above sea level. Peak elevation is at the 0.4 km mark.

Start and end points: back (or north) entrance of Melbourne Zoo, 50 metres from Royal Park Station. The halfway point is CERES.

Be alert: Road crossings at Poplar Rd, Bowen Crescent, Lygon St (traffic lights), Amess St, Nicholson St (traffic lights), Rae St, Brunswick St, St Georges Rd, Bennett St.

Try to spot: An old railway station that has been converted o a community centre.

Navigation tips: From the Melbourne Zoo back gate, get onto the Capital City Trail just outside Royal Park Station. At 0.6 km, there is a triple fork, take the middle one that goes to a tunnel under Royal Parade. At 3.5 km, take the left fork (Merri Creek Trail). At 4.2 km, you will reach St Georges Rd. Cross the creek via St Georges Rd and go under the road when you reach the other side of the creek. At 5.7 km, the south gate of CERES is on your left. Retrace your steps to go back to the start.

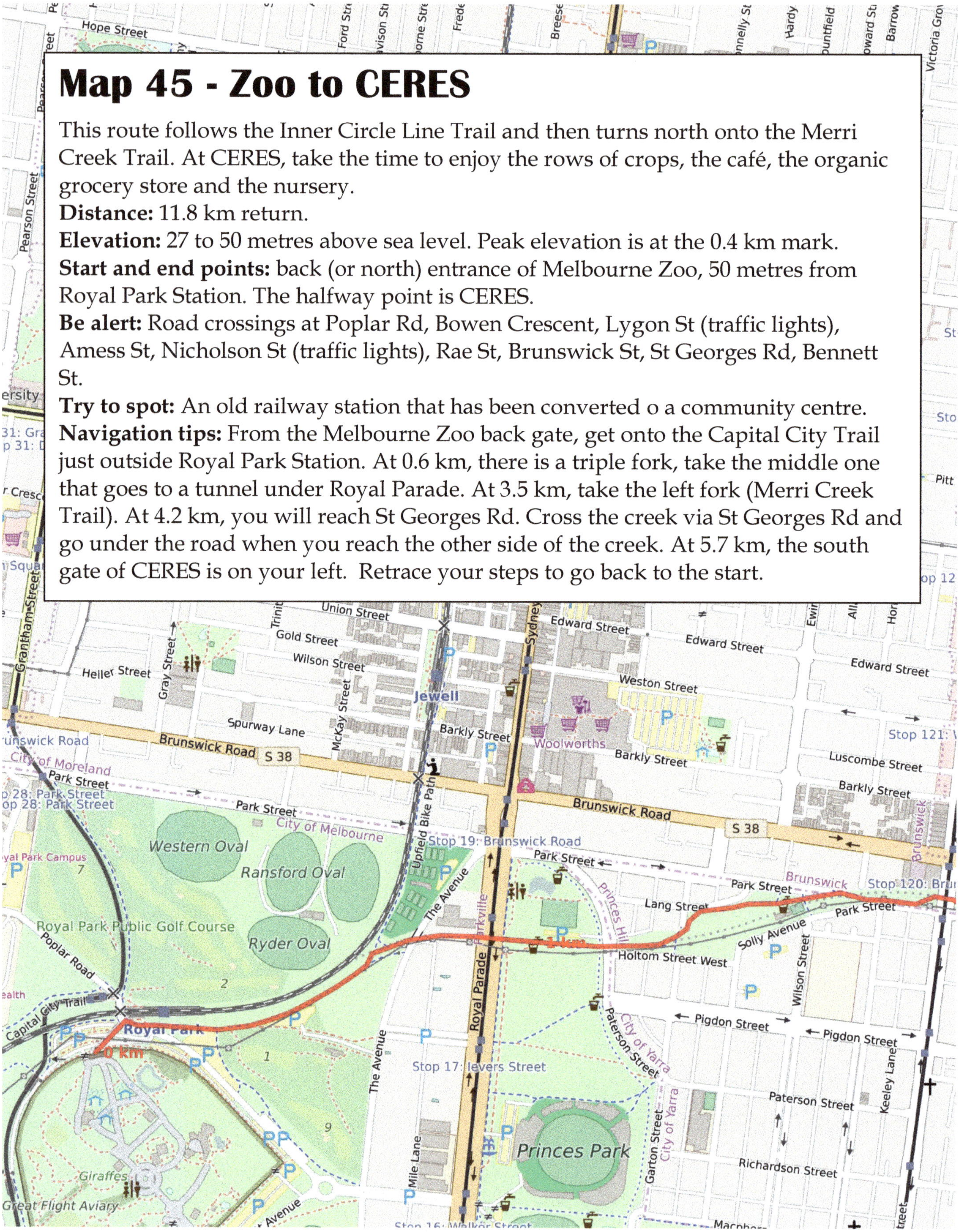

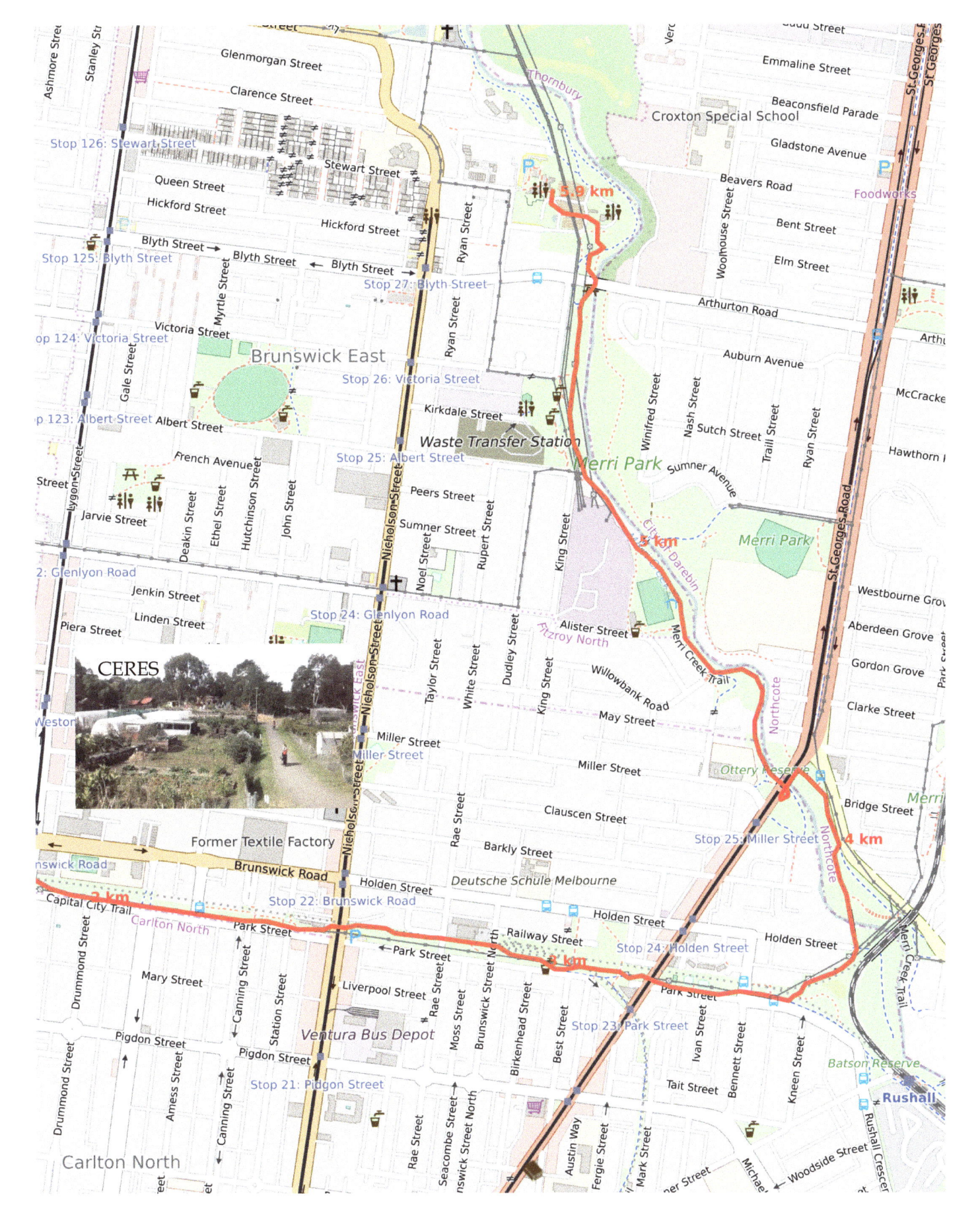

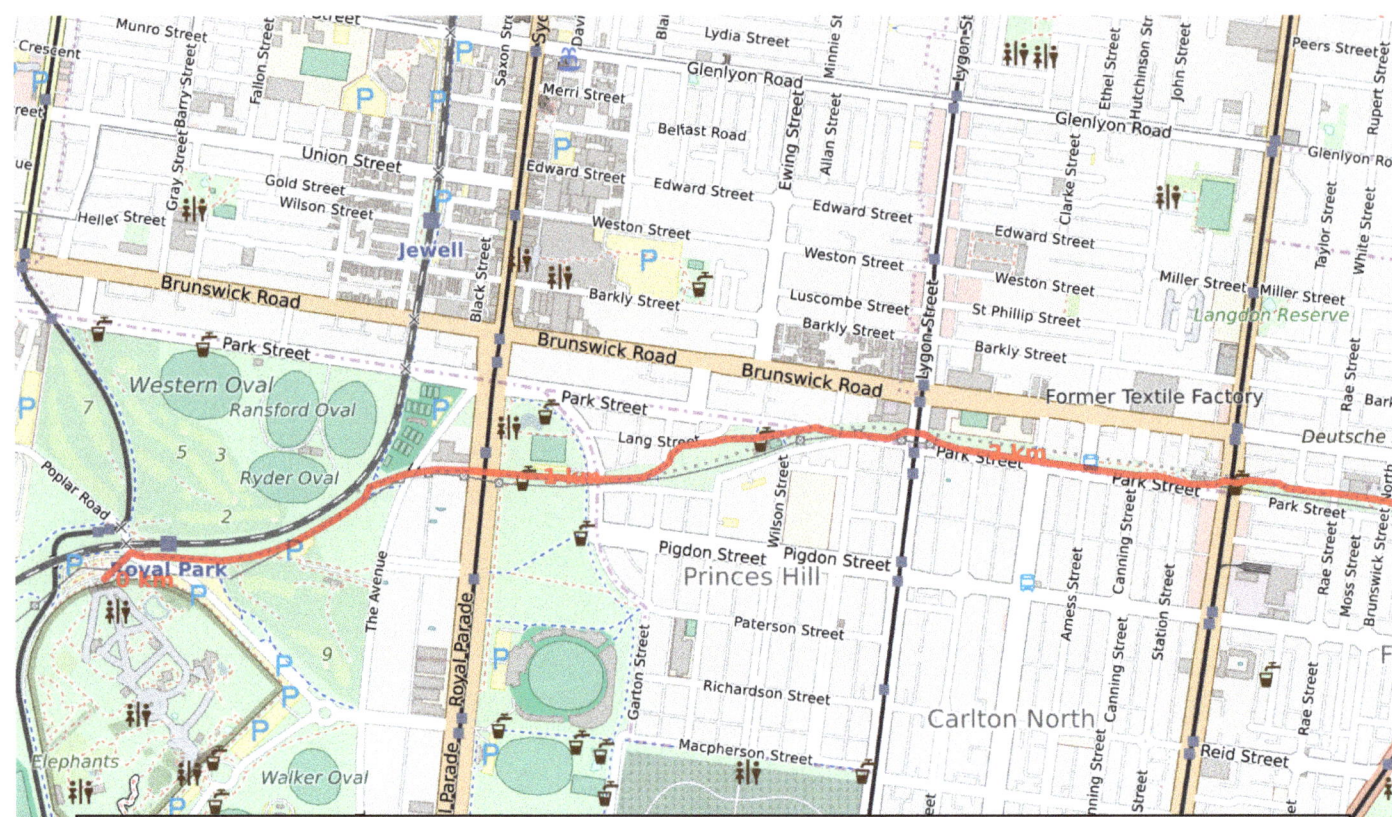

Map 46 - Zoo to Fairfield Boathouse

This trail follows the Capital City Trail closely. Don't forget to have tea and scones at Fairfield Boathouse.

Distance: 6.7 km one-way (13.4 km return)
Elevation: 17 to 50 metres above sea level. Peak elevation is at the 0.4 km mark.
Start point: Melbourne Zoo back gate (north side), 100 metres from Royal Park Station.
End point: Fairfield Boathouse, 500 metres from Dennis Station.
Be alert: Road crossings at Poplar Rd, Bowen Crescent, Lygon St (traffic lights), Amess St, Nicholson St (traffic lights), Rae St, Brunswick St, St Georges Rd, Bennett St, Yarra Bend Rd
Try to spot: A defunct railway station turned to a community centre.
Navigation tips: From the Melbourne Zoo back gate, get onto the Capital City Trail just outside Royal Park Station. At 0.6 km, there is a triple fork, take the middle one that goes to a tunnel under Royal Parade. At 3.5 km, there is a fork but continue straight. At 3.8 km, cross the train tracks at Rushall Station by going through the tunnel. At 5.3 km, go under Heidelberg Rd and go uphill and cross Merri Creek via Heidelberg Rd. When you are on the eastern side of the creek, join the trail again on the right. At 6.1 km, take the left fork and cross Yarra Bend Rd. At 6.5 km, you will see the carpark for Fairfield Boathouse. Enjoy some coffees at the Boathouse before returning to the start, or you can go to the nearest train station (Denis Station).

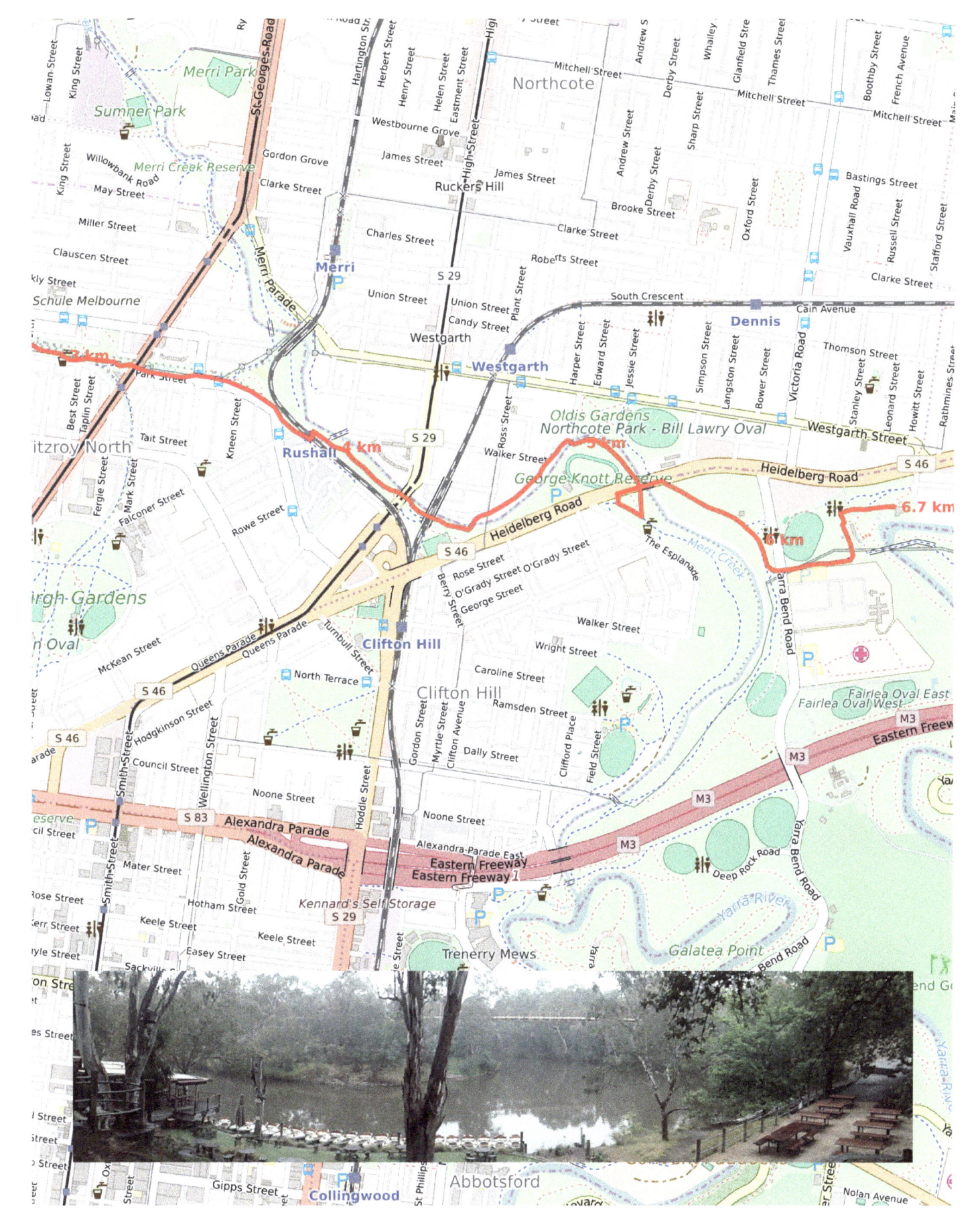

Map 47 - City to Zoo

Melbourne Zoo is surprisingly close to the CBD but I've chosen a longer way which is more scenic. The route detours into Docklands and goes under the CityLink Tollway for at least one kilometre.

Distance: 9.0 km one-way (18.0 km return)

Elevation: 1 to 37 metres above sea level. Peak Elevation is at the zoo.

Start point: Flinders Street Station

End point: The back gate of the zoo, near Royal Park Railway Station and trams 19 & 58.

Be alert: Road crossings at Queensbridge St (traffic lights), Spencer St (traffic lights), Navigation Dr, Collins St (traffic lights), Bourke St (traffic lights), Observation Dr, Footscray Rd (traffic lights), exit road from Citylink (traffic lights), Poplar Rd

Try to spot: Melbourne International Gateway artwork, Melbourne Zoo

Navigation tips: From Federation Square, walk down Princes Bridge and turn left to go under Princes Bridge. You are now on the south bank of the Yarra River. Walk westwards until the 2.3 km mark, where you cross Webb Bridge to Docklands. Walk along Harbour Esplanade until the 3.5 km mark, then turn left to walk along the water. At 4.0 km, turn right and walk through Harbour Town Shopping Centre. Go around the Melbourne Star (ferris wheel). At 4.8 km, cross Footscray Rd and walk along Moonee Ponds Creek. At 7.6 km, ascend the path up to Flemington Bridge Station and continue north-eastwards along the Capital City Trail. When you hit Poplar Rd, the zoo is only a short distance to your right.

View from Flemington Bridge Railway Station

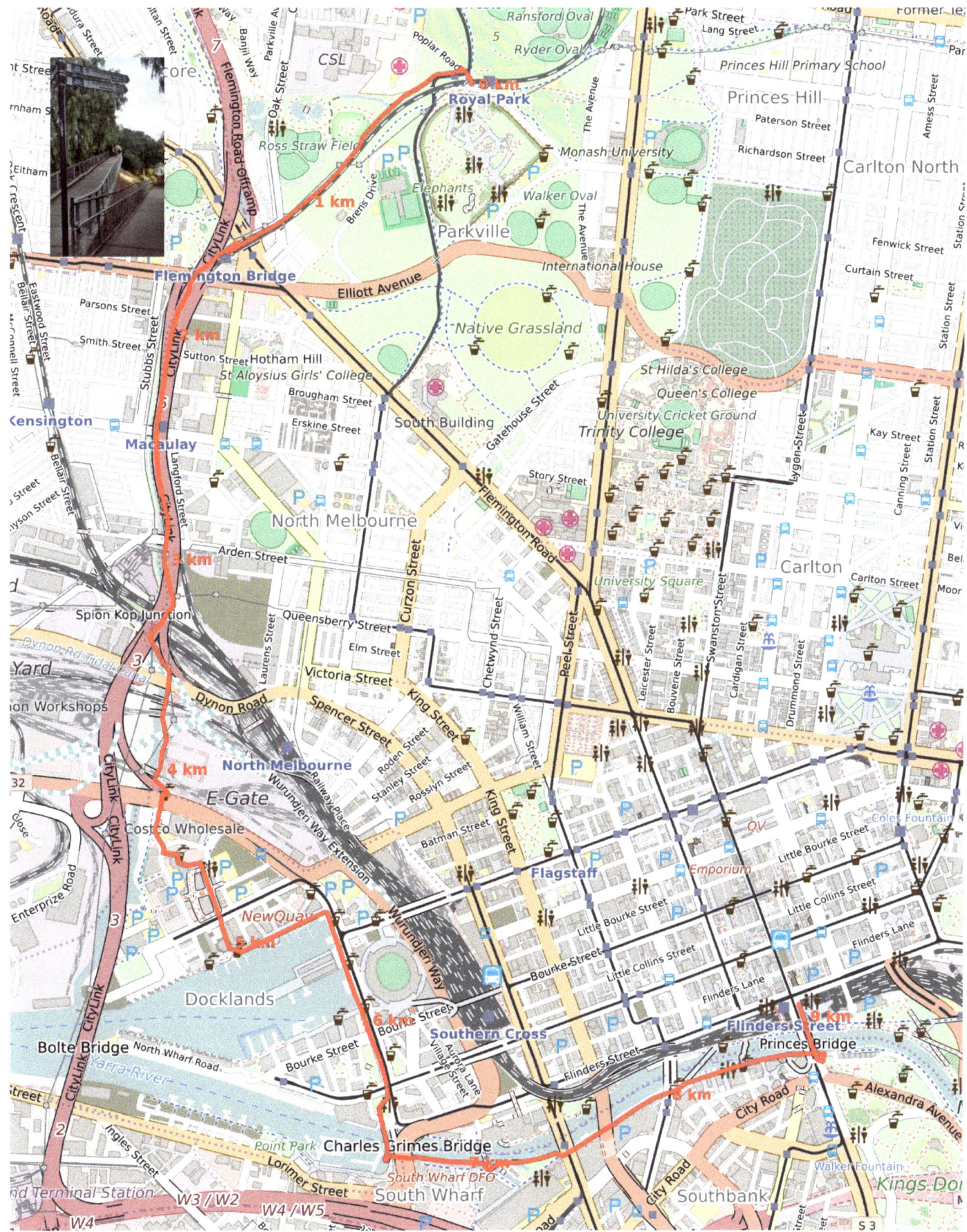

Map 48 - Rushall Station to City

This track uses the Capital City Trail and follows Merri Creek (pictured below) and the Yarra River. Fun Fact: There is a song called 'Rushall Station' by indie Melbourne band, Underground Lovers.

Distance: 16.6 km one-way (33.2 km return)
Elevation: 1 to 34 metres above sea level. Peak elevation is at 6.0 km.
Start point: Rushall Station   **End point:** Flinders Street Station
Be alert: No road crossings!
Try to spot: Collingwood Farm, Rod Laver Arena
Navigation tips: From the carpark area outside Rushall Station, go through the tunnel to get to the other side and follow Merri Creek. At 1.4 km, cross under Heidelberg Rd and go up a steep slope and go left (head south-east). At 2.4 km, take the left fork and at 2.7 km, cross the footbridge and turn right (westwards), At 3.0 km, turn right and cross the footbridge over Merri Creek. At 4.2 km you will reach Collingwood Farm. At 5.1 km, climb the stairs and cross the footbridge. Turn right at 5.3 km and you will be walking along Yarra Boulevard. At 6.0 km, take the right fork. At 6.4 km, cross the footbridge and continue to follow the Yarra River downstream. Hug the north bank of the Yarra from now on and you will reach Federation Square. For variety, you can also go on the south bank of the Yarra, from the 12th km onwards.

Merri Creek

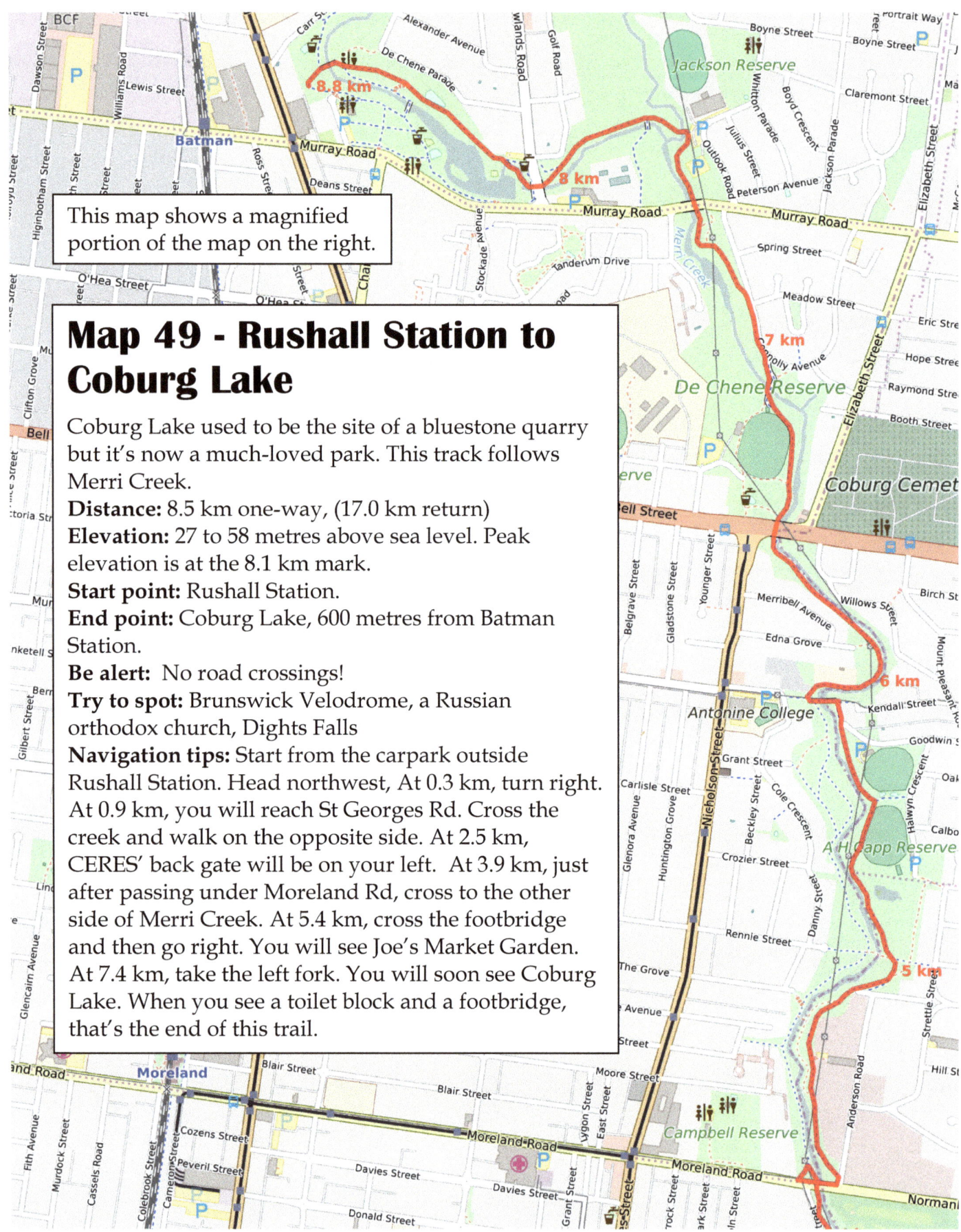

This map shows a magnified portion of the map on the right.

Map 49 - Rushall Station to Coburg Lake

Coburg Lake used to be the site of a bluestone quarry but it's now a much-loved park. This track follows Merri Creek.

Distance: 8.5 km one-way, (17.0 km return)
Elevation: 27 to 58 metres above sea level. Peak elevation is at the 8.1 km mark.
Start point: Rushall Station.
End point: Coburg Lake, 600 metres from Batman Station.
Be alert: No road crossings!
Try to spot: Brunswick Velodrome, a Russian orthodox church, Dights Falls
Navigation tips: Start from the carpark outside Rushall Station. Head northwest, At 0.3 km, turn right. At 0.9 km, you will reach St Georges Rd. Cross the creek and walk on the opposite side. At 2.5 km, CERES' back gate will be on your left. At 3.9 km, just after passing under Moreland Rd, cross to the other side of Merri Creek. At 5.4 km, cross the footbridge and then go right. You will see Joe's Market Garden. At 7.4 km, take the left fork. You will soon see Coburg Lake. When you see a toilet block and a footbridge, that's the end of this trail.

Map 50 - Epping to Alphington

This track follows the Darebin Creek, which starts in Wollert and flows 50km to Alphington where it joins the Yarra.

Distance: 22.4 km one-way (44.8 return)
Elevation: 34 to 127 metres above sea level. Peak elevation is at the start.
Start point: Epping Station
End point: Alphington Station
Be alert: Road crossings at the entry road to Epping Station, Hendersons Rd, Childs Rd, McKimmies Rd, Settlement Rd, Chenies St, Yarana Rd, Wingrove St
Navigation tips: From Epping Station, go east along Cooper St. At 0.3 km, cross Hendersons Rd and get onto the Darebin Creek Trail. At 2.5 km, cross Childs Rd and pick up the trail 100 metres to the east. At 4.2 km, you will reach McKimmies Rd. Move 100 metres westwards and there should be an island in the middle of the road where you can cross. At 5.9 km, you will reach the Metropolitan Ring Rd. Go east for 900 metres and you will find a tunnel to go under the Ring Rd. At 11.6 km, the trail reaches the end of Rathcowen Rd and stops. Walk westwards along Rathcowen Rd for 600 metres then pick up the trail again. At 12.8 km, cross to the other side of the creek. At 14.1 km, cross to the other side of the creek using Plenty Rd. At 17.4 km, at a cross junction, go right (westwards). At 21.8 km, keep going straight at the fork. You will soon reach Alphington Station.

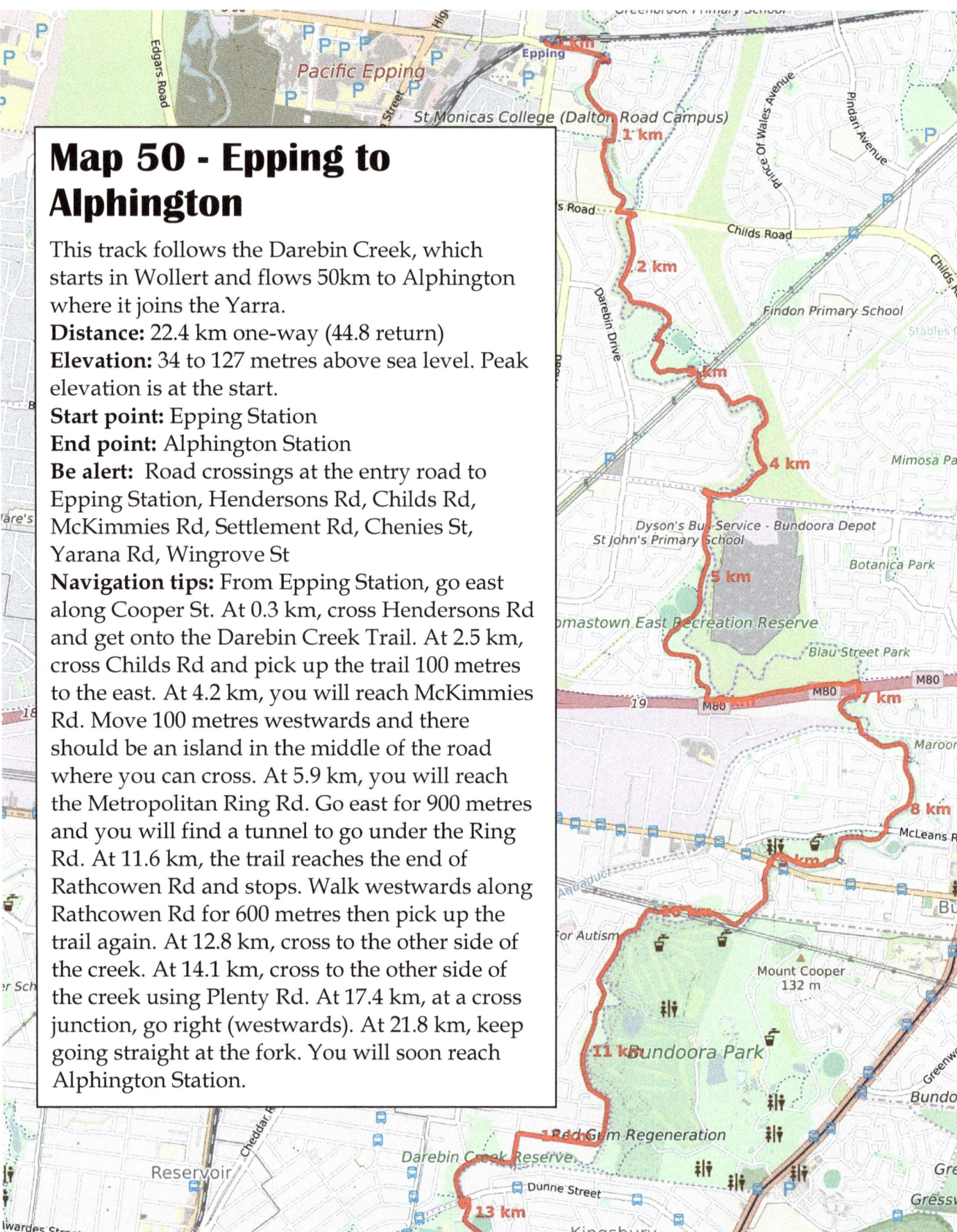

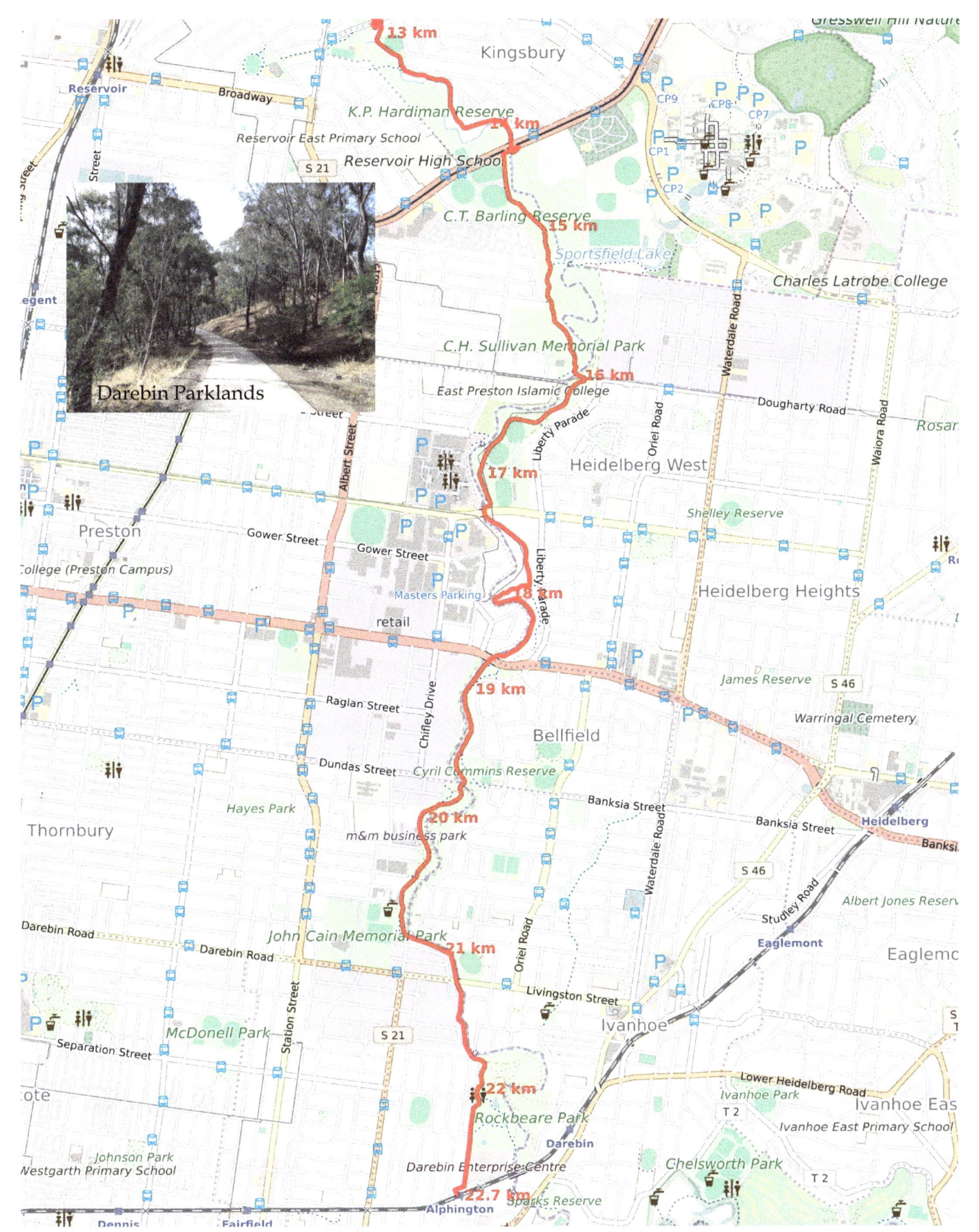

Map 51 - Alphington to City

This track uses the Darebin Yarra Trail that was opened in 2018 and joins it with the Main Yarra Trail. **Distance:** 21.4 km one-way (42.8 km return)
Elevation: 1 to 49 metres above sea level. Peak elevation is at the 5.4 km mark.
Start point: Alphington Station.   **End point:** Flinders Street Station.
Be alert: Road crossing at Yarra Bend Rd.
Navigation tips: From Alphington Station, walk north along Yarana Rd. At 0.4 km, turn right into the Darebin Parklands. At 0.6 km, turn right again and follow this trail to the 3.0 km mark where you will reach the Main Yarra Trail. Go right (westwards) and follow this trail all the way to the city. At 4.8 km, you will pass under the Chandler Highway and go up stairs to walk westwards along Yarra Boulevard. At 5.4 km, turn right, leave Yarra Boulevard and follow a descending track to the pipe bridge. After crossing the bridge, turn right and left (follow the Main Yarra Trail signs). At 6.5 km, cross Yarra Bend Rd and turn left. At 7.8 km, turn right and cross the footbridge over Merri Creek. At 9.9 km, go up the stairs and cross the footbridge then turn right. At 10.8 km, turn right, leave Yarra Boulevard and go downhill. At 11.3 km, cross the footbridge and continue eastwards. From now on, walk on this side of the Yarra River all the way to Federation Square.

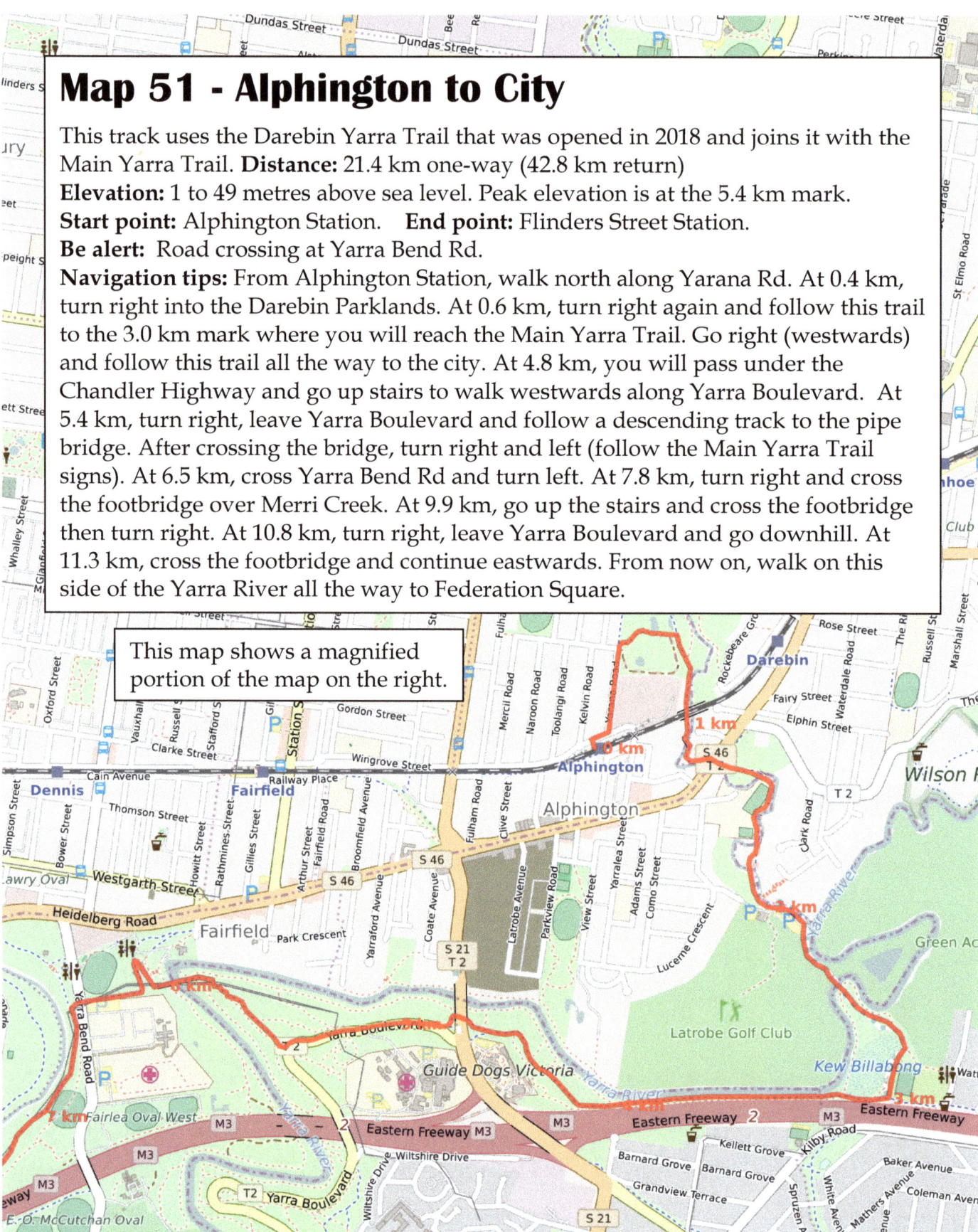

This map shows a magnified portion of the map on the right.

112

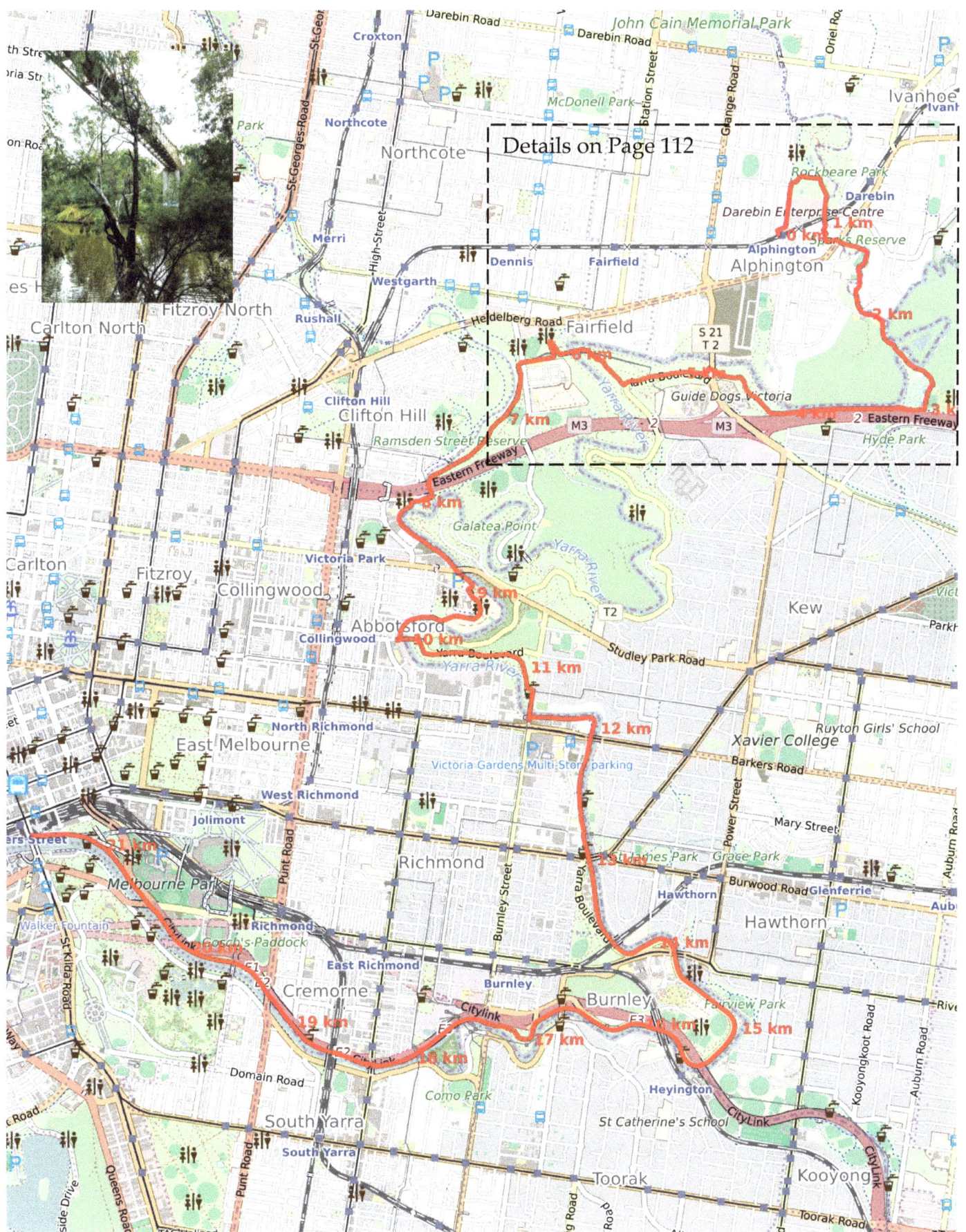

Map 52 - Epping Marathon

This marathon goes from Epping all the way down to the Federation Square. It is a combination of the tracks in Maps 50 (north part) and 51 (south part). For more map details, do study the entirety of Maps 50 and 51. A convenient half-way exit point for this walk is Alphington Station.
Distance: 42.6 km one-way.
Elevation: 1 to 127 metres above sea level. Peak elevation is at the start.
Start point: Epping Station
End point: Flinders Street Station
Be alert: See Maps 50 and 51
Try to spot: See Maps 50 and 51
Navigation tips: See Maps 50 and 51

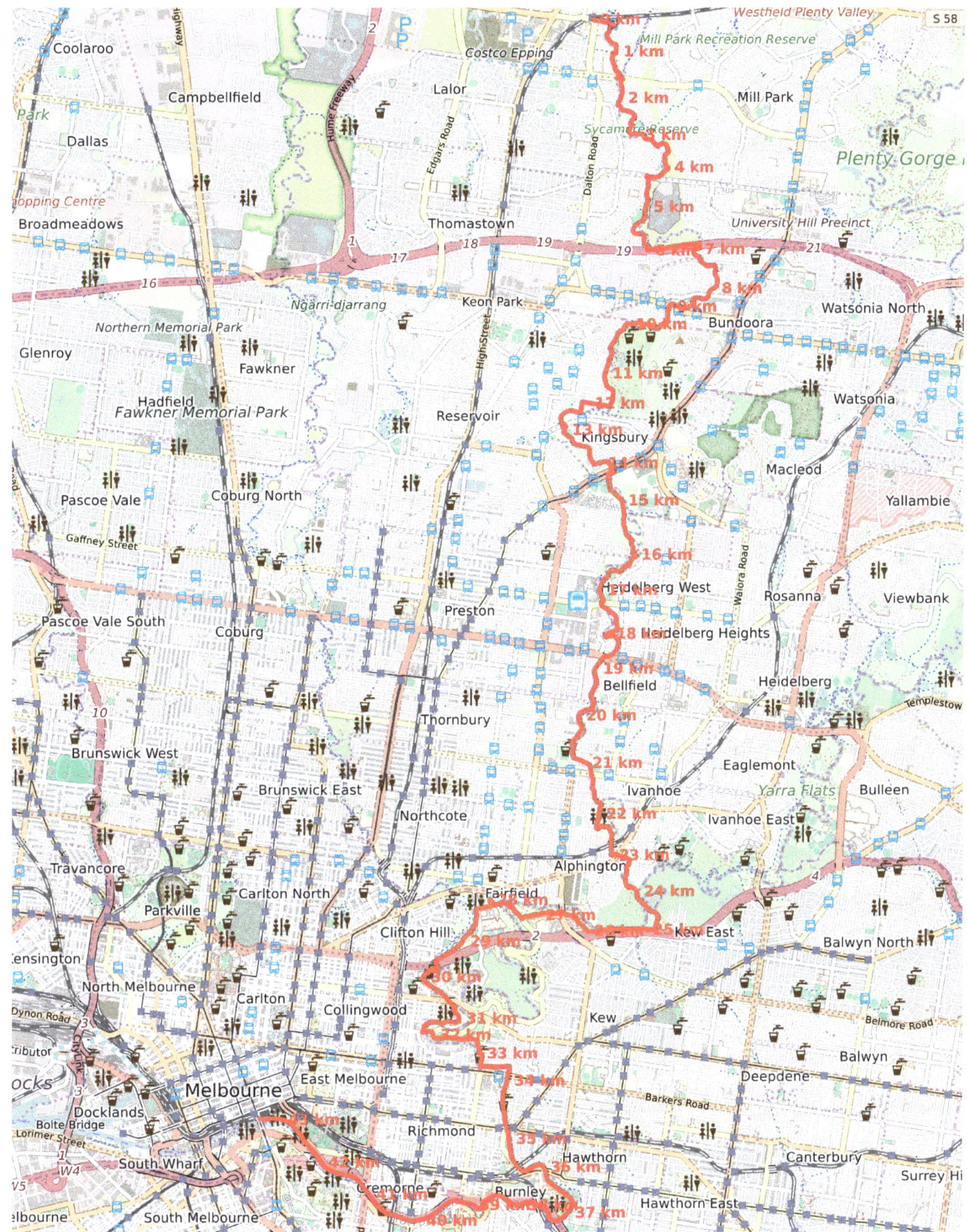

End Notes

Thank you for reading this book. I hope you will enjoy the trails as much as my walking group does. I look forward to hearing your feedback about the trails. And do look out for Volume 2!

To learn more and to communicate with me, please visit these links:

Marathon Walking Facebook Page
www.facebook.com/marathonwalking

My walking group's schedule of walks in Melbourne:
www.meetup.com/Marathon-Walking-Community
If you are ever in Melbourne, join us for a walk!

Marathon Walking Instagram page
www.instagram.com/marathonwalking

Also written by me: *Marathon Training for Walkers and Beginners*
If you are an avid walker and want to challenge yourself by walking 42 km marathons, you might be interested in this book!
amzn.to/2CxOjNq

Photo Credits

https://commons.wikimedia.org/wiki/File:Princes_Park,_Carlton_North,_Victoria,_Australia.jpg
Mat Connolley (Matnkat) [GFDL (http://www.gnu.org/copyleft/fdl.html), CC-BY-SA-3.0 (http://creativecommons.org/licenses/by-sa/3.0/) or CC BY 2.5 (https://creativecommons.org/licenses/by/2.5)], from Wikimedia Commons

https://commons.wikimedia.org/wiki/File:South_Melbourne_market_outside_1a.jpg
Commander Keane / CC BY-SA (https://creativecommons.org/licenses/by-sa/3.0)

https://upload.wikimedia.org/wikipedia/commons/8/8d/Simple_compass_rose.svg
Brosen, modification by Howcheng [GFDL (http://www.gnu.org/copyleft/fdl.html) or CC BY 3.0 (https://creativecommons.org/licenses/by/3.0)], via Wikimedia Commons

Map legend

 Water fountain or tap (for drinking)

 Public toilet

 Picnic facility

 Viewing point

 Monument

 Museum

 Fountain (decorative)

 Bus stop

 Train station or tram stop

 Railroad crossing

 Carpark

 Park

 Cycling track

 Footpath or multi-use track

 Railway line

 Tram line

 Freeway

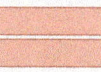 Highway

 Primary road

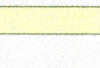 Secondary road

 Residential road

 One-way road

 River or canal

 Stream or drain

www.ingramcontent.com/pod-product-compliance
Lightning Source LLC
Chambersburg PA
CBHW040751020526
44118CB00042B/2857